The Anointing: the Vital Ingredient

Trevor Newport

New Wine Press

New Wine Press
PO Box 17
Chichester
England PO20 6YB

All Scripture quotations are taken from the King James Version – Crown
copyright.

ISBN: 1 874367 89 2

Typeset by CRB Associates, Reepham, Norfolk.
Printed in England by Clays Ltd, St Ives plc.

Contents

Chapter 1

Introduction

Throughout my Christian life and ministry I have become more and more aware that the Holy Spirit can flow in so many different and diverse ways. Many have come to understand that these various manifestations of the Third Person of the Trinity are called 'Anointings'.

I have discovered that there are manifold anointings for all kinds of activities in the kingdom of God, and the reason for this book is to heighten our awareness of these anointings to enable us all to become much more sensitive to them and thus be more fruitful. The other thing to realise about a particular anointing is that it can change as time goes by. This is why many people become stale and many movements become monuments of what used to be. This book will hopefully help you to stay fresh in your calling and so enable you to maintain a high level of anointing throughout your Christian life, which will impact the world around you for the better.

> *'But the anointing which ye have received of him abideth in you, and ye need not that any man teach you: but as the same anointing teacheth you of all things, and is truth, and is no lie, and even as it hath taught you, ye shall abide in him.'*
>
> (1 John 2:27)

This verse seems to suggest that we all receive a general anointing which stays (abides) in us. This is true of course, but I would strongly suggest that this general anointing takes on many different facets through each of us, rather like the 'fruit' (singular) of the Spirit which consists of at least nine individual manifestations (Galatians 5:22, 23). I say, 'at least', since there are six other manifestations of the Spirit mentioned in the New Testament. Therefore, from one fruit we have no less than 15 manifestations in each of us through Jesus Christ. Hallelujah! These are all different anointings in themselves.

Some people are anointed to do a specific task for a season only and then it lifts off them. This needs to be carefully noted because there is nothing worse than a person trying to do something without the anointing. However, it happens all too often. This is where leadership is needed to help the body of Christ to full maturity, by ensuring that everyone is fulfilling their calling within the body, thus producing the maximum corporate anointing possible.

I trust that this book will significantly help to prevent you from being embarrassed in any way, by eliminating anything in your life which is not anointed, **so freeing you to do only what you are anointed for at this present time**. Hopefully, you will be challenged, convicted, encouraged and led into a deeper walk with the Anointed One, the **Lord Jesus Christ**!

Chapter 2

First Encounter
with the Anointing

If you were brought up in Christian home then you were surrounded by a certain degree of anointing from birth. This is both a privilege and an awesome responsibility.

Luke 12:48 says:

> *'But he that knew not, and did commit things worthy of stripes, shall be beaten with few stripes. For unto whomsoever much is given, of him shall be much required: and to whom men have committed much, of him they will ask the more.'*

This is therefore very true of the many who have such an upbringing. This is the same as the Jews of old who had the law and commandments. The anointing was there for them at all times but they still managed to backslide. Unfortunately, so it is with many who have the chance to know the Lord from an early age and yet rebel against Him for various reasons.

However, many other people are not so fortunate. I, for one, was brought up without the knowledge of God in a non-Christian home. There was a bit of religion but nothing alive in the Spirit. Consequently, since the darkness hates the Light I did not want to know about the things of God whenever I came into contact with true Christianity.

It took a strong anointing from a strong Christian man to get through to me when I was 19 years old. I resisted the anointing coming from him for many months but eventually realised that I needed Jesus Christ the Anointed One in

my life. My life completely changed as soon as I allowed
God's life, power and anointing to enter me fully. I wanted
everything that the Lord had to offer. I had exhausted the
world and all it had to offer and now I was ready to serve
God with my whole being. This was my first encounter with
the Anointing of the Holy Spirit. One of the first things that
happened in me was a revelation of **love** towards people
that I had never known before. Also, I saw creation in a
completely new light – trees, plants, flowers etc. It was as if it
had all come alive. The anointing had taken the scales off my
eyes for the first time and I was so different.

'I once was dead but now I am alive, was blind but now I
see.' Hallelujah!

Thus my first encounter with the Anointing was being
born again. This was the most dramatic act of God in my life
to date, even though I have since seen angels and had all
kinds of spiritual experiences with God.

John 3:3 says:

> *'Jesus answered and said unto him, Verily, verily, I say unto*
> *thee, Except a man be born again, he cannot see the kingdom*
> *of God.'*

Born again means born from above, born anew, or born
from **the top**. Therefore, when you were born again you were
literally born from the top, or **from the highest level of**
anointing!

I want to mention something very important about our
Lord and Saviour, Jesus Christ. The word 'Christ' is defined as
'the Anointed and His Anointing' according to one translation. The *Strong's Concordance* simply says 'Anointed'.

Either way Jesus Christ is literally Jesus the Anointed One.
This is why your life changes so much because He comes to
live inside of you and His anointing starts to work on you in
all sorts of ways.

I would like to address all of you who have been Christians
for a long time. The anointing of God still wants to be at
work in your life as we are changed from one level of glory to
another. He still has work for you to do and it is up to you
to keep the anointing fresh upon you. I will be explaining
how to do that as we go along. We all need a fresh anointing

in our lives since the very act of living saps it away! A regular encounter with the Lord keeps this alive! I believe that the anointing upon our lives should really grow stronger as we go on and not diminish in any way.

Chapter 3

The Baptism in the Holy Spirit

Once we are born again we immediately become a candidate for the baptism in the Holy Spirit with the evidence of speaking with new tongues. This adds a whole new dimension to the anointing! Praise the Lord!

I had been a Christian for a whole year before I was taught properly from Scripture about this wonderful experience. Jesus said when He was on the earth that He would go to heaven and send the Holy Spirit down to the earth to help us throughout life.

Luke 24:49 says:

> *'And, behold, I send the promise of my Father upon you: but tarry ye in the city of Jerusalem, until ye be endued with power from on high.'*

John 14:26 says:

> *'But the Comforter, which is the Holy Ghost, whom the Father will send in my name, he shall teach you all things, and bring all things to your remembrance, whatsoever I have said unto you.'*

John 15:26 says:

> *'But when the Comforter is come, whom I will send unto you from the Father, even the Spirit of truth, which proceedeth from the Father, he shall testify of me.'*

Over the years I have been amazed at how many people there are in 'so called' Pentecostal, charismatic churches, who are still not baptised in the Holy Spirit. Many years ago I was in one of the largest Pentecostal denominations in Britain and part of my job involved travelling around and speaking in other churches within that group of churches. It had been mightily used of God many years ago in signs, wonders, healings etc. but sadly it had slowly lost its power. I would often go into these churches and ask the congregation how many had experienced the baptism of the Holy Spirit and to my astonishment there would be hardly any who spoke in tongues. They had lost this particular anointing and it certainly showed in the meetings! I told one such church off for it and was told never to return. I am glad because I did not want to go back either. In fact I don't think God goes to it any more. If we want to keep the anointing of God strong upon the church then we need this precious baptism of the Spirit.

A few weeks ago, when I was in America, I visited a certain Full Gospel church for the first time. I could tell that it was slipping back into traditions and so I asked them how many were **not** filled with the Spirit with the evidence of speaking in tongues. There were 19 people who put their hands up and so we prayed. Sixteen came through speaking in tongues straight away with two young girls and an elderly gentleman who did not. The two girls had sin in their lives and needed to repent. The gentleman wanted to know why he was not coming through and so I asked the Lord for a word of knowledge. The Lord spoke to me that he was a freemason and so I challenged him about it and sure enough he was! The anointing for the baptism in the Spirit will not be released into anyone's life who is into the occult. This man did not know and so I told him to renounce it and to go home and burn all his freemasonry material which he promised to do. After only five seconds he was speaking in tongues and praising God after waiting 25 years!

Thus it is important to remember that things can hinder any aspect of the anointing in our lives and so we need to be on our guard. Also we, as leaders, need to name such things as freemasonry etc., so that the people we are called to serve can have a chance to enjoy all the blessings of the gospel. We use a deliverance questionnaire which shows most things that stop the flow of the Spirit in our lives. Please feel free to order a copy at our ministry address at the back of this book.

One of the main reasons for this baptism is to empower us for evangelism. Acts 1:8 says:

> *'But ye shall receive power, after that the Holy Ghost is come upon you: and ye shall be witnesses unto me both in Jerusalem, and in all Judaea, and in Samaria, and unto the uttermost part of the earth.'*

I had been a Christian for a whole year before I was filled with the Spirit and spoke in tongues. I had tried to share my faith with people but knew that something was missing. I was sad because nobody accepted Jesus into their hearts even though I tried so hard. Then after I had received this baptism I started leading people to Christ with effortless ease and realised the power of this experience. I have since led thousands of people to Jesus Christ through personal evangelism and preaching. The anointing for winning souls has increased steadily over the years. In fact in the last two years I have on several occasions had the joy of seeing hundreds of people accepting Christ at one time. To God be all the glory!

There is unique anointing released whenever I share the way of salvation with people. I can feel God's pleasure whenever I witness to unsaved people, particularly when they accept it fully. This is eternal work which saves a soul from hell-fire, and has the potential for that person to become a soul winner themselves. The devil attacks personal evangelism above most things because of this awesome impact on a person's life. Be a soul winner and just watch the anointing grow upon your life!

Mark 16:15 says:

> *'And he said unto them, Go ye into all the world, and preach the gospel to every creature.'*

Another reason for this baptism is to assist our prayer life. 1 Corinthians 14:14 says:

> *'For if I pray in an unknown tongue, my spirit prayeth, but my understanding is unfruitful.'*

Romans 8:26 says:

'Likewise the Spirit also helpeth our infirmities: for we know not what we should pray for as we ought: but the Spirit itself maketh intercession for us with groanings which cannot be uttered.'

If you would like further help in this area then please order our booklet on *How to Pray in the Spirit.*

Then there are the spiritual gifts which are available to every believer as soon as they are baptised in the Holy Spirit. 1 Corinthians 12:1 says:

'Now concerning spiritual gifts, brethren, I would not have you ignorant.'

1 Corinthians 12:4 says:

'Now there are diversities of gifts, but the same Spirit.'

1 Corinthians 12:9 says:

'To another faith by the same Spirit; to another the gifts of healing by the same Spirit.'

1 Corinthians 14:1 says:

'Follow after charity, and desire spiritual gifts, but rather that ye may prophesy.'

1 Corinthians 14:12 says:

'Even so ye, forasmuch as ye are zealous of spiritual gifts, seek that ye may excel to the edifying of the church.'

When I first found out about these supernatural gifts I decided to ask for all of them! These gifts release such a powerful anointing into the life of the church that I realised it was imperative that I understood about their function and operation. During the first few years of ministry the Lord was gracious with me by releasing these gifts in stages so that I could get used to the anointing for each gift. Later in this book we will look at the different anointings for each gift.

Another reason for the baptism in the Holy Spirit is to assist us in worship. Look what Paul says:

> *'What is it then? I will pray with the spirit, and I will pray with the understanding also: I will sing with the spirit, and I will sing with the understanding also.'*
>
> (1 Corinthians 14:15)

Once we have received this baptism in the Spirit and are able to speak in tongues we can use these tongues to 'sing in the spirit' as Paul says here. This is a wonderful experience and helps us to draw close to God in the heavenly languages, which in turn releases a fresh anointing into our spirit. This in turn helps to release the spiritual gifts in us to help minister to others in prophecy, healing etc. I have seen a greater concentration of miracles through high praise and worship than almost anything else. Having said this, I do not want to take anyone's attention away from preaching the Word which is very important. I believe that we need both to maximise the anointing in public meetings.

Baptism in Water

Mark 1:10 says:

> *'And straightway coming up out of the water, he saw the heavens opened, and the Spirit like a dove descending upon him.'*

This is where Jesus was baptised in water by John the Baptist. Once we have accepted Jesus Christ as our Lord and personal Saviour we then need to be baptised in water just like Jesus Himself who set us all an example to follow in His footsteps. It is a step of necessary obedience and all who seek to go on with God need to be baptised in water by full immersion. It is an outward demonstration and testimony to others that the inward change has already taken place. An anointing for obedience is immediately released, thus enabling us to continue in this marvellous adventure of the Christian life. Study these scriptures carefully:

> *'He that believeth and is baptised shall be saved; but he that believeth not shall be damned.'*   (Mark 16:16)

'Then Peter said unto them, Repent, and be baptised every one of you in the name of Jesus Christ for the remission of sins, and ye shall receive the gift of the Holy Ghost.' (Acts 2:38)

'Then they that gladly received his word were baptised: and the same day there were added unto them about three thousand souls.' (Acts 2:41)

'And he commanded them to be baptised in the name of the Lord. Then prayed they him to tarry certain days.'

(Acts 10:48)

If you read through the Acts of the Apostles you will see that believers were baptised in water very soon after they accepted Jesus as Saviour. It is a command from God Himself which we all need to submit to. If you have not been baptised in water since you were saved then ask your pastor or leaders to arrange it for you and **be blessed**!

Chapter 4

The Anointing
upon the Word of God

Whenever you spend time in the Word of God you are opening yourself up to receive a fresh anointing from His precious Word. I am often reduced to tears when I read the Scriptures, as His tangible presence anoints me simply through soaking up His Word. It is awesome. The Word is so powerful! His Word changes us just as we read it and allow it to invade our lives.

The Bible is self-anointed! It is God's word to man and is as if He is speaking to you directly. He has given us His Word which is complete in every way. Thank God for His Word. Read His Word every day. Speak it out loud. Proclaim it with authority. The whole corporate power of Heaven is behind His Word.

> *'Every word of God is pure: he is a shield unto them that put their trust in him.'* (Proverbs 30:5)

> *'So then faith cometh by hearing, and hearing by the word of God.'* (Romans 10:17)

> *'And take the helmet of salvation, and the sword of the Spirit, which is the word of God.'* (Ephesians 6:17)

> *'For this cause also thank we God without ceasing, because, when ye received the word of God which ye heard of us, ye received it not as the word of men, but as it is in truth, the word of God, which effectually worketh also in you that believe.'* (1 Thessalonians 2:13)

*'For the word of God is quick, and powerful, and sharper than
any two-edged sword, piercing even to the dividing asunder of
soul and spirit, and of the joints and marrow, and is a
discerner of the thoughts and intents of the heart.'*

(Hebrews 4:12)

*'All Scripture is given by inspiration of God, and is profitable
for doctrine, for reproof, for correction, for instruction in
righteousness.'*   (2 Timothy 3:16)

Thus if we spend time apart from the Word of God by
being too busy doing other things, the anointing that we
receive from the Word will dissipate and we will feel 'flat' and
dry. The outcome of this is that our faith level will decrease.
The only way to prevent this from happening is to stay in the
Word at all times as we are continually exhorted to do.
Joshua 1:8 says:

*'This book of the law shall not depart out of thy mouth; but
thou shalt meditate therein day and night, that thou mayest
observe to do according to all that is written therein: for then
thou shalt make thy way prosperous, and then thou shalt
have good success.'*

Do you want good success in life? Do you want to
experience continual prosperity? Then spend much quality
time in your Bible. Read it and read it and read it again, and
just watch the anointing contained in the Word grow in you
and your capacity to receive from God increase all the time.
There is no anointing quite like it.

Confession of the Word

If you have a problem in your life then you can use God's
Word to help solve that problem, whatever it is. For example,
if you need healing for your body then find all the healing
scriptures you can and start to confess them out loud until
healing comes. You see, there is an anointing for healing
contained in the scriptures on healing! Many have missed
this, and they run to this preacher and that preacher, and
all the time they could have been healed simply through
their Bibles. I am not saying that every condition can be

healed this way, but most can. I do this all the time to keep me well.

There are some situations that need someone else to help if there has been a long-standing problem. Some people need to be set free from curses or spirits of infirmity which need to be discerned. This is why God anoints people within the body of Christ with certain gifts. The Lord uses me to bring healing to people in every church I go to. In fact, I am in Tasmania at the moment in Australia, and I was ministering last night to a church and gave an appeal for healing, and the anointing was so strong for healing that one lady was healed before I touched her! After I had prayed for all the people I asked how many had been healed straight away and just about everyone had been healed. Praise God! This is the healing anointing which I have sought for many years. This year I have seen a greater anointing for healing than ever before. The anointing grows upon our lives and ministries as we are faithful to the call of God.

It does not just work in the area of healing but any area mentioned in the Word. If you are struggling in the area of finances then you need to get the scriptures out regarding finances, and confess them out loud until victory comes. I do this all the time and keep increasing.

Here are a few scriptures to start with:

> *'And he shall be like a tree planted by the rivers of water, that bringeth forth his fruit in his season; his leaf also shall not wither; and whatsoever he doeth shall prosper.'*
>
> (Psalm 1:3)

> *'Beloved, I wish above all things that thou mayest prosper and be in health, even as thy soul prospereth.'*   (3 John 1:2)

> *'If they obey and serve him, they shall spend their days in prosperity, and their years in pleasures.'*   (Job 36:11)

> *'Let them shout for joy, and be glad, that favour my righteous cause: yea, let them say continually, Let the Lord be magnified, which hath pleasure in the prosperity of his servant.'*   (Psalm 35:27)

'But seek ye first the kingdom of God, and his righteousness; and all these things shall be added unto you.'

(Matthew 6:33)

'But thou shalt remember the LORD thy God: for it is he that giveth thee power to get wealth, that he may establish his covenant which he sware unto thy fathers, as it is this day.'
(Deuteronomy 8:18)

The Lord desires for you to prosper in every area of life so that you can fulfil your destiny and calling upon earth. The difference between prosperity and materialism is that prosperity says, 'How can I give?' but materialism says, 'How can I get?'

These two are totally opposite. A prosperous person is able to feed the poor, send out missionaries, build buildings and fund the gospel. There is nothing worse than wanting to be able to bless someone and not being able to. I believe that there is an anointing in God's Word to enable us to prosper through giving, where we can meet our own needs and those of others, and so speed up the work of God on the earth. Poverty is a curse! Christ Jesus came to set us free from all curses including poverty. As I travel around the world I still meet a poverty mentality wherever I go and so I continue to teach against it. Proverbs 11:24 says:

'There is that scattereth, and yet increaseth; and there is that withholdeth more than is meet, but it tendeth to poverty.'

Be a giver and **be blessed**!

Are you struggling in any other area of life? If so, then find out what God's powerful Word has to say about it and spend some quality time reading and meditating on it, until the anointing is released through the Word to meet that situation. It works for marriage, victory over temptation and the devil, developing a sound mind, applying the Word to your work situation and anything else that life challenges us with. There is victory for us in the anointed Word for every day, every situation and every problem.

'But thanks be to God, which giveth us the victory through our Lord Jesus Christ.'　　　　(1 Corinthians 15:57)

'For whatsoever is born of God overcometh the world: and this is the victory that overcometh the world, even our faith.'

(1 John 5:4)

The Word of God is **highly anointed**! Therefore, spend much quality time soaking up its pages every day of your life and just watch your spiritual life grow.

Chapter 5

Different Anointings

There are different anointings for different things as we shall now discuss.

Personal Evangelism

When I first became a Christian I knew that part of my responsibility was to share my faith with others. This is both a command and a great joy. Mark 16:15 says:

'And he said unto them, Go ye into all the world, and preach the gospel to every creature.'

1 Peter 3:15 says:

'But sanctify the Lord God in your hearts: and be ready always to give an answer to every man that asketh you a reason of the hope that is in you with meekness and fear.'

I have found that there is a unique anointing upon me whenever I share my faith with someone who is lost. When I was at university in Liverpool I used to pray a simple prayer asking the Lord to arrange for me to witness to one person each day. As I prayed this every morning I began to experience one divine appointment after another. I would find myself sitting next to someone and before long I would be sharing my faith with them. After a while I found that it became easier and easier the more I did it. I started to feel a tangible anointing come upon me whenever I talked to people about eternal issues. It kept me fresh and focused on really important issues.

When I first began to witness I would try to talk to everybody I met and found that many were not interested. Then, the more I persevered, the anointing of the Holy Spirit would lead me to the right people and I became much more Spirit-led as to who I would talk to. It was so exciting! Why not start today?

I find now that the anointing for personal evangelism is so well established in me that God can call upon me any time, anywhere. I remember one time when I was in Australia. I had just finished preaching in Tasmania and was flying to the mainland to continue ministering in Adelaide. My flight time was only about one hour. They served us the little plastic meal and announced that we were descending into Melbourne. As we started our descent the young man sitting next to me leaned across to me and asked me what I was doing in Tasmania. I was quite tired and wanted to rest but I decided to share my faith with him. He was 21 years old and yet had never heard the gospel before! He became more and more interested and so I asked him if he wanted to accept Jesus Christ into his heart and repent of his sin. He said yes. I only had about one minute from start to finish but he was born again before we landed!

This happens to me regularly these days because God knows that I will do my job. Last year I saw no less than 700 people come to know Christ Jesus as Saviour either through preaching or personal evangelism. The anointing is growing all the time! There is no joy like leading someone to Jesus Christ. It is wonderful.

Luke 10:2 says:

> *'Therefore said he unto them, The harvest truly is great, but the labourers are few: pray ye therefore the Lord of the harvest, that he would send forth labourers into his harvest.'*

I pray that you will take up the challenge today to be a personal evangelist and see the anointing grow upon your life with life-changing results.

Proverbs 11:30 says:

> *'The fruit of the righteous is a tree of life; and he that winneth souls is wise.'*

Breaking of Bread

Whenever you come around the communion table to partake of the bread and the fruit of the vine, you are remembering the New Covenant and what Jesus Christ did for you on the cross. This service is very special. There is a unique anointing released to all believers who share in it. Luke 22 says:

> 'And he took the cup, and gave thanks, and said, Take this, and divide it among yourselves. For I say unto you, I will not drink of the fruit of the vine, until the kingdom of God shall come. And he took bread, and gave thanks, and brake it, and gave unto them, saying, This is my body which is given for you: this do in remembrance of me. Likewise also the cup after supper, saying, This cup is the new testament in my blood, which is shed for you.'　　　　　(Luke 22:17–20)

1 Corinthians 11 says:

> 'After the same manner also he took the cup, when he had supped, saying, This cup is the new testament in my blood: this do ye, as oft as ye drink it, in remembrance of me. For as often as ye eat this bread, and drink this cup, ye do shew the Lord's death till he come. Wherefore whosoever shall eat this bread, and drink this cup of the Lord, unworthily, shall be guilty of the body and blood of the Lord; But let a man examine himself, and so let him eat of that bread, and drink of that cup. For he that eateth and drinketh unworthily, eateth and drinketh damnation to himself, not discerning the Lord's body. For this cause many are weak and sickly among you, and many sleep. For if we would judge ourselves, we should not be judged. But when we are judged, we are chastened of the Lord, that we should not be condemned with the world.'　　　(1 Corinthians 11:25–32)

This is therefore a very serious anointing. It brings the responsibility of walking right with God in the face of us all. It means that we should forgive one another before sharing in it. If we have sinned then we should repent before breaking bread.

Note: You don't have to wait until the communion table

before repenting of any sin. Repent as soon as you realise you have sinned. We should come to the table of remembrance in victory as a celebration of what Jesus Christ did for us 2000 years ago.

In some services around the world, the people are reminded constantly of their past sins and they have to confess them every time they break bread. This is absurd since the Blood of Jesus Christ has already cleansed us from them. This develops a sin consciousness which is very negative. The Scriptures declare to us that:

> *'For sin shall not have dominion over you: for ye are not under the law, but under grace.'*   (Romans 6:14)

This is good news for us all. Once you have repented of sin it is finished! The Blood of Jesus has cleansed it. Why go on magnifying all our previous sins all over again every week? The devil must often laugh at this ignorance!

> *'If we confess our sins, he is faithful and just to forgive us our sins, and to cleanse us from all unrighteousness.'*
>
> (1 John 1:9)

We are only to confess sins once. Previously confessed sins have been long since forgiven. Praise God! Jesus came to set us free from sin, not to push our face in it all the time. Every sin that you have committed both prior to conversion and after you were saved, has been forgiven, provided that you have repented and turned away from each of them. This is the grace of God.

Take a look at David's struggle with sin after his worst mistakes with Bathsheba and Uriah:

> *'Hide thy face from my sins, and blot out all mine iniquities. Create in me a clean heart, O God; and renew a right spirit within me. Cast me not away from thy presence; and take not thy holy spirit from me. Restore unto me the joy of thy salvation; and uphold me with thy free spirit.'*
>
> (Psalm 51:9–12)

David knew that the anointing of God had left him and he desperately wanted it to be restored. This is the power of turning away from sin. The freshness of the anointing is marred when we sin and so we should seek to maintain a true walk with the Lord and repent speedily if we sin.

Incidentally, sin has degrees. By this I mean that some sins have serious consequences like this example with David. Not only had he committed adultery with Bathsheba but he had arranged the death of Uriah her husband as well. These are extremely serious sins and God was so displeased with David that the anointing of God upon his life was withheld for a season as a disciplinary measure. David needed to see the severity of his sin which caused much ammunition for the enemies of God. Sin opens the door for the enemy to attack us. Thus the anointing acts as a shield of protection for us.

Jesus taught us that all sin needs to be repented of but that some are more serious than others because of the consequences. For instance, Jesus said that murder and hate were equal as far as sins are concerned but murder has far more lasting consequences which are outward instead of inward. Jesus also used the illustration of adultery and lusting after someone in your heart. They are both sins but one is outward with long-lasting consequences, and the other is inward which can lead to more serious sins.

David was deeply repentant after his sin and cried out to God for the restoration of their fellowship and the anointing that such a relationship brings.

Psalm 51 is there to remind us all that however close we are to the Lord, we can still fall into sin if we do not keep our guard up at all times. The Lord will always give us warnings if we get too close to a sinful situation, and we would be very wise to take heed to those warnings and prevent similar disasters.

Chapter 6

How to be
Anointed Above Others!

Hebrews 1:9 says:

> *'Thou hast loved righteousness, and hated iniquity; therefore
> God, even thy God, hath anointed thee with the oil of
> gladness above thy fellows.'*

This verse is obviously talking about our precious Lord and
Saviour Jesus Christ but He is our example in all things and
so the same must apply to us. There is a way to be anointed
above our fellows!

The vital ingredient of the anointing has been sadly
lacking in so many people's lives because we have not taken
holiness seriously enough. We have not hated sin as much as
we should.

I once heard an interesting illustration about sin which is
worthy of quoting. Imagine a road high up in the hills with a
sheer drop on the edge of the road. Many people walk close
to the edge of sin instead of on the other side of the road,
where there is no chance of sinning. Some people go as close
up to sin as they think they can get away with, but sadly, as is
often the case, they fall off the edge and sin. We have all been
guilty of this and need to be on our constant guard against it
all the time. We have an enemy who delights to see godly
people fall into sin. He likes nothing more than to gloat over
a Christian who has fallen into sin. Sin causes shame, hurts,
distrust, resentment etc. It gives the enemy so much un-
necessary ammunition against us. Let us all make a quality

decision to live as far away from sin as possible; away from the edge where it is safe and secure. Joseph had the right attitude towards Potiphar's wife and stayed as far away from her as he could. As I read in Scripture about this story it seems that Joseph was totally innocent. She was so determined to defile Joseph sexually but he kept fleeing from her. We need the same attitude today even if we get falsely accused. Read the story again for yourself (Genesis 39).

Read the following scriptures:

> *'The righteous also shall hold on his way, and he that hath clean hands shall be stronger and stronger.'*   (Job 17:9)

> *'Who shall ascend into the hill of the LORD? or who shall stand in his holy place? He that hath clean hands, and a pure heart; who hath not lifted up his soul unto vanity, nor sworn deceitfully. He shall receive the blessing from the LORD, and righteousness from the God of his salvation.'*
>
> (Psalm 24:3–5)

> *'Having therefore these promises, dearly beloved, let us cleanse ourselves from all filthiness of the flesh and spirit, perfecting holiness in the fear of God.'*   (2 Corinthians 7:1)

> *'But as he which hath called you is holy, so be ye holy in all manner of conversation. Because it is written, Be ye holy; for I am holy.'*   (1 Peter 1:15–16)

Thus we are to be holy as God Himself is holy. That is our goal. Another interesting verse which tests just how holy we are in our thought life is this:

> *'**Unto the pure all things are pure:** but unto them that are defiled and unbelieving is nothing pure; but even their mind and conscience is defiled.'*   (Titus 1:15)

Have you ever been in conversation with someone and you say something which could be twisted to mean something else? Some people are like that about everything. They have a corrupt mind and defile every pure conversation. How is your mind? Does your mind twist things around to mean something different? If so, then you need to change your thought life. Our minds need to be spring-cleaned and purified to think pure things. This is not just about unclean things but other things as well. Some people have a suspicious mind, while others have minds which are too curious. Let us be pure in every area of our thought life and see the anointing grow.

> *'Finally, brethren, whatsoever things are **true**, whatsoever things are **honest**, whatsoever things are **just**, whatsoever things are **pure**, whatsoever things are **lovely**, whatsoever things are of **good report**; if there be **any virtue**, and if there be **any praise**, **think on these things**.'*
>
> (Philippians 4:8)

Thus we have a choice as to what we think about! The devil tries to play tricks on our mind but we can choose not to allow those things to fester and cause us to sin.

This is all to do with the anointing by the way! Many have this false idea that they can live any way they want to and still expect the anointing to flow. Some go to this meeting or that meeting in search of the anointing or a fresh touch from God. Whenever the next 'big name' comes through town certain people are sure to be there in the hope of getting the anointing. I am not advocating that we should not go to these meetings. On the contrary I think we should! However, we should go with a different attitude. Whenever we see someone operating in a strong anointing we should be challenged to pay the same kind of cost that that person has made instead of trying to get his or her anointing. Second-hand anointings are short lived! Why not spend more time in the presence of the Almighty for yourself, hungering for a personal breakthrough into higher ground. You will find as you spend quality time with the Father that any sin that has crept into your life will soon show up, which will cause you to repent of the negative in order for a fresh anointing to come. Seek God for yourself instead of relying on others for it!

I challenge you to seek God so much that the next time a big meeting comes along you go to it **with** the anointing, instead of **for** the anointing!

The tangible, penetrating, holy anointing of God is available to every Christian. I have experienced His presence many times over the years but I hunger for more! I have had a taste and it causes me to want more. I have seen heaven opened, angels visiting me, spent hours weeping as the presence of God overwhelms me **but I want more**. I have had seasons of fasting and prayer over the years to draw close to God and have experienced His divine presence so many times but I hunger for **more and more and more** of Him!

> *'As the hart panteth after the water brooks, so panteth my soul after thee, O God.'* (Psalm 42:1)

We need a renewed passion for the presence of God. I don't care how long you have been a Christian. Do you have an up-to-date fresh relationship with Him? Have you grown stale, stagnant and dull in your spiritual life? Are you hearing from God like you used to or does His voice seem strangely dim? You need to take time out and seek Him like never before.

Pay the price of godliness. When was the last time you spent a couple of days fasting? I have always found that there is no substitute for prayer and fasting. (We have books on prayer and fasting. Please write to us if you would like a book catalogue.) Hebrews 12:14 says:

> *'Follow peace with all men, **and holiness, without which no man shall see the Lord.'***

The word *'see'* in this verse has a very interesting meaning in the Greek. It means 'to gaze **with wide-open eyes, as at something remarkable'**; as opposed to simply voluntary observation or merely mechanical, passive or casual vision. It signifies an earnest but more continued inspection.

Therefore, holiness causes our eyes to be fully open to be able to gaze upon The Lord Himself with wide open eyes to behold His wonderful face in all His glory.

One of the finest passages of Scripture to help us to understand holiness is found in Psalm 15, which says:

> *'LORD, who shall abide in thy tabernacle? Who shall dwell in thy holy hill? He that walketh uprightly, and worketh right-eousness, and speaketh the truth in his heart. He that backbiteth not with his tongue, nor doeth evil to his neigh-bour, nor taketh up a reproach against his neighbour. In whose eyes a vile person is despised; but he honoureth them*

> *who fear the LORD; he that sweareth to his own hurt, and*
> *changeth not. He that putteth not out his money to interest,*
> *nor taketh reward against the innocent. He that doeth these*
> *things shall never be moved.'*   (Psalm 15:1–5)

These are the things that cause the anointing in our lives either to diminish or increase. In other words it is how we live.

We have choices to make every single day of our lives that will cause the Holy Spirit's anointing to be attracted to us or the opposite. God has given us the choice therefore as to how anointed we become.

The Holy Spirit

Have you ever wondered why the Third Person of the Trinity is called the **Holy** Spirit? If He was in heaven He would only need to be referred to as the Spirit. But on earth He has the title **Holy** Spirit because sin dwells on earth. Thus the Holy Spirit is attracted to Holy vessels upon the earth. He is not attracted to but repelled by unclean vessels.

We know from Scripture that God is no respecter of persons and not partial in any way. Therefore, those who are more anointed have paid the necessary price. In other words, when we get our act together as believers, the Holy Spirit will anoint us to do great things in the Kingdom. Daniel 11:32 says:

> *'And such as do wickedly against the covenant shall he*
> *corrupt by flatteries: but the people that do know their God*
> *shall be strong, and do exploits.'*

I personally believe that, since the Lord knows how weak we are in the flesh, He graciously bestows an ever increasing anointing upon us in stages. Study the following verses:

> *'I the LORD search the heart, I try the reins, even to give every*
> *man according to his ways, and according to the fruit of his*
> *doings.'*   (Jeremiah 17:10)

> *'The steps of a good man are ordered by the LORD: and he*
> *delighteth in his way.'*   (Psalm 37:23)

> *'For promotion cometh neither from the east, nor from the west, nor from the south. But God is the judge: he putteth down one, and setteth up another.'*   (Psalm 75:6–7)

Some people never seem to put a foot wrong in the kingdom and are progressively promoted. Most of us go through the fires of affliction, often through our own making, and learn from our mistakes. Many seem to go through a wilderness prior to doing some great work in the kingdom – for example, Moses or Joseph. We are all very different and have to have all kinds of things shaved off us in order to be ready for the Master's hand of service. Sadly, there are many who do not seem to come through the Father's shaping process and become cynical and critical. This is sad but true.

Another aspect of preparation is something that none of us really enjoys.

Persecution

I don't know anyone who gets excited about this subject but it is here to stay if you want a strong anointing. In fact, the stronger the anointing (need I say it), **the greater the persecution!**

The amazing thing about persecution is that we usually get persecuted for doing what is right – I can almost hear many of you laughing to yourself right now. Let us look at the Word of God.

> *'Blessed are they which are persecuted for righteousness' sake: for theirs is the kingdom of heaven. Blessed are ye, when men shall revile you, and persecute you, and shall say all manner of evil against you falsely, for my sake. Rejoice, and be exceeding glad: for great is your reward in heaven: for so persecuted they the prophets which were before you.'*

(Matthew 5:10–12)

> *'Remember the word that I said unto you, The servant is not greater than his lord. If they have persecuted me, they will also persecute you; if they have kept my saying, they will keep yours also.'*   (John 15:20)

> *'And have no root in themselves, and so endure but for a time: afterward, when affliction or persecution ariseth for the word's sake, immediately they are offended.'*   (Mark 4:17)

> *'Yea, and all that will live godly in Christ Jesus shall suffer persecution.'*   (2 Timothy 3:12)

If you are preaching the truth of God's Word you will receive persecution for it. This is a promise of God. What you must do is stand up for the truth. Don't ever back off from persecution – that is what the enemy wants you to do. I have made the decision in my own life that every time someone comes against me for preaching something, I preach it more. I have taken the stand that if I get resistance then it is doing some good! Every so often I get attacked for preaching certain subjects, in particular the subjects of healing, faith, prosperity and deliverance. These four subjects seem to provoke a reaction more than anything else! Consequently, you will often hear me preach on these subjects.

Incidentally, persecution is not just from people! It is often religious spirits speaking through people but there is another aspect of persecution that I want to mention. I will discuss this in the next chapter.

Chapter 7

Direct Assault from Hell

It is one thing to be persecuted through people but it is something else when hell directs a missile straight at you! You see, the devil knows how you are coping through his attacks. If you are getting stronger through his attacks then he will change strategy. Satan is after the anointing upon us because it is the anointing that destroys bondages in people's lives and invades the enemy's camp, thus advancing the kingdom of God.

Isaiah 10:27 says:

> *'And it shall come to pass in that day, that his burden shall be taken away from off thy shoulder, and his yoke from off thy neck, and **the yoke shall be destroyed because of the anointing.'***

While we are in this Earth we shall have to fight against the powers of darkness. There is no easy route. Remove the idea from your thinking that it is glamorous to carry a strong anointing. It isn't glamorous at all. It is **war**!

I remember when we took over our present building in the centre of Stoke-on-Trent. The very place that the Father wanted us to be and the very last place that Satan wanted.

The first few months were warfare all the time. I had to deal with many territorial spirits coming against me, but now I am so glad that the Lord allows me to see them coming!

One night I saw a horrible looking creature coming towards me in the corridors of Bemersley House. It did not know that I could see him. I asked the Lord what his name was and the Holy Spirit told me that his name was Apollyon. He had come to destroy our church. The name Apollyon means 'destroyer'. I bound this demon in the Name of Jesus Christ and told him to leave. He was shocked when he realised that I could see him. He left after a few minutes and I then saw this demon go up to a chief spirit to report what had happened. This chief spirit then assigned a special demon to attack Life Changing Ministries. I saw all this going on in vision form. The following night I was in prayer with Peter Watkins in our buildings late at night (the Lord had shown me to do it at night). During our time of prayer this special satanic agent came up to me and tried to attack me. I was ready for him and gave him the shock of his life! He went back to the chief overseer and I saw him say 'I am never going back there.' He never has to this day. Even if he dared to I would be ready for him.

Matthew 11:12 says:

> *'And from the days of John the Baptist until now the kingdom of heaven suffereth violence, and the violent take it by force.'*

We have to fight for all kinds of things in the kingdom because we are promised opposition. It is when we fight for something that we become established in the anointing in that area of life.

If ever you see someone with a strong anointing in any area of ministry then you know that they have had to go through some battle grounds to get where they are. Make a decision to be a fighter for truth and increase in the anointing.

I have often observed in my life that I go through an increased season of persecution before a new breakthrough comes. In fact, once I realise what is happening, I begin to rejoice because I know from the increased attacks that the Lord is about to do something good on my behalf. This is very motivating and I recommend it as a good attitude to adopt.

It is as if the enemy finds out that God is about to bless us in some way and so he attacks with one of his usual missiles. I remember going on a recent trip to America. As soon as I boarded the plane I was attacked with a 'flu bug. It was the worst attack I had had for many years. I had to fight off this sickness for about 17 days, which is very unusual for me. However, I soon realised one of the reasons for this attack was due to some wonderful breakthroughs in the ministry for me. I did not miss one meeting even though I was quite weak at times. The anointing was stronger than I had ever known and many more doors have opened for me.

A Prophet without Honour

Matthew 13:57 says:

> *'And they were offended in him.* **But Jesus said unto them, A prophet is not without honour, save in his own country, and in his own house.'**

I never really appreciated or understood this verse of Scripture until I began to travel abroad. The truth is that we have no honour in our own country, our own church or our own family. You just have to live with this fact. I have struggled many times with the fact that the people that you minister to in your own fellowship are often the ones that appreciate you the least. It is always a shock for me whenever I come home from foreign lands back to my own church, and realise the absence of honour.

The way I see it is that we are anointed with a unique substance which we will call 'the honour anointing'. I have been amazed when I have been preaching the same message abroad as I would in my own church back home. I remember one day in Singapore when I was asked to speak in a bank at lunch time. This particular bank has so many Christians in it that they close at lunch time every day so that they can have a meeting. I preached to about 60 that day and heaven opened. Many were weeping as the Holy Spirit was poured out. It was nothing to do with me. It was everything to do with the honour anointing.

2 Corinthians 12:15 says:

> *'And I will very gladly spend and be spent for you; though the more abundantly I love you, the less I be loved.'*

I have certainly proved this verse many times! The people that we have helped the most are often those that show us the least respect. In fact I would describe the role of a pastor as that of a doormat. A place for people to wipe their feet on and walk straight over you! In every church I have pastored I could count on one hand the people who have appreciated my ministry. No wonder nobody wants to be a pastor. If the Lord had not been with me over the years I doubt very much if I would still be doing it. He has been the greatest source of encouragement. I will never forget one evening I had preached my socks off and felt good to have discharged my responsibility again. Nobody said anything. I went home and as I walked into the lounge The Lord spoke to me and said, 'Thank you.' Those words meant so much to me. Praise His name!

Why not learn from this and say a big heartfelt thank you to your pastor now and again. It means so much and costs nothing.

Chapter 8

Obedience
Increases the Anointing

Jeremiah 7:23 says:

> *'But this thing commanded I them, saying, **Obey my voice,**
> and I will be your God, and ye shall be my people: **and walk
> ye in all the ways that I have commanded you, that it
> may be well unto you.'***

Jeremiah 7:24 says:

> *'But they hearkened not, nor inclined their ear, but walked in
> the counsels and in the imagination of their evil heart, and
> went backward, and not forward.'*

If I was asked what the one thing was above all else that
causes the anointing to grow in our lives, I would have to say
obedience. It is the main key to success in the Christian life.

We are going to look at different aspects of obedience.

Preaching What the Lord Commands

The sure way to guarantee the anointing in preaching is to
live holy and upright before the Lord and to **obey** exactly
what He says. I was once talking to a colleague in ministry
and we were talking about preaching. He told me that the
Lord had given him a word to preach that Sunday evening. I
saw him on the Monday and asked him if he had preached
the word that God had given him and he said '**no**'! I was so
shocked that someone would disobey God so casually. I can

honestly say before the Lord that I have always preached what He has given me. He always gives me a word to preach and I always preach it without compromise. How could I grow in the anointing for preaching without absolute obedience? Nothing else would be anointed as far as I am concerned. You may as well tell a few nursery rhymes as not preach the Word of God. Both would be equally flat.

I think this is where preachers need some serious talking to. The Lord God Almighty is a Dictator. He is always right. How dare you ever preach anything other than what He gives you! His word is a command from Heaven itself. When you preach the Word that He gives you it **will always be anointed**! Simple obedience to His Word guarantees the anointing on your preaching, even if the people don't like it. Their reaction is no measuring stick of the anointing. You may be preaching to religious-minded bigots! Anything anointed would upset them. Jesus had to say some hot stuff to many who would hear Him.

I was once asked to go to a Pentecostal church that must remain nameless. The Lord said to me that this was their last time before He would remove their lampstand. I was shocked. The Lord told me to preach against hypocrisy etc. I was only a young man at the time and found myself saying some really hard things. It was pretty obvious that the Spirit of God had not moved for a long time because it was so dead. The following day I had a telephone call from the pastor (he was away that night preaching elsewhere). He had been there for 15 years. He gave me a right telling off for upsetting 'his' people. Many of them had phoned up complaining that I had been asked to speak. I had preached the Word of God. I later heard that within just three weeks the pastor left the church and fled to London. It is a very serious thing to obey God at all times.

I have walked into churches at times and the Lord has said some awesome things to me about either the whole church or individuals. I keep my word to the Lord which I have vowed, and always speak what He gives me. I have recently been to a city in the world that many preachers have been thrown out of. I have now joined them. One church there has vowed never to have me back. The feeling is mutual. The anointing has a profound impact on people. Some will love you for obeying and others will want to stone you! Either way you must obey.

Hebrews 4:12 says:

> *'For the word of God is quick, and powerful, and sharper than any two-edged sword, piercing even to the dividing asunder of soul and spirit, and of the joints and marrow, and is a discerner of the thoughts and intents of the heart.'*

Thus, whatever reaction you may receive from people, keep preaching what the Lord gives to you and the anointing upon your preaching will increase.

Luke 16:10 says:

> *'He that is faithful in that which is least is faithful also in much: and he that is unjust in the least is unjust also in much.'*

You will also notice that the size of your congregation will begin to grow as well! I started out as a young pastor with just eight people to preach to five times a week. I was only 21 years old and felt overwhelmed with that responsibility. In the last few years the size of audience has rapidly increased. I recently spoke to 2500 in one meeting and the anointing was awesome. I gave an appeal for people to respond to Jesus as Saviour and 356 first-time decisions were recorded. I prayed for the sick and cast out demons and hundreds were healed and set free.

When I was first in ministry I would be extremely nervous until I actually started speaking and then the anointing would calm me down. Now I don't get nervous at all. I have grown out of it because of the anointing. Praise God.

I was going through a very difficult time in the ministry many years ago and I was due to preach twice the following day which was the Sunday. I was overwhelmed by a situation that made me feel incapable of ministering. This was the Saturday night. All of a sudden the Lord spoke to me and said these words: 'Son, every time you preach I send two special angels to stand by your side. I am **not** going to send these angels tomorrow...' There was a pause while I went into shock! He then continued, 'I am going to send **My Son** to stand with you instead!' The Lord knew exactly what I was going through and those words have kept me going many times since.

Another thing about the anointing upon preaching is this: if the words that you are saying are not anointed then they will not reach into the people's spirits. They will forget it quickly and not have been fed that day. However, every time you preach the Word that God gives you, it will invade the entire congregation and penetrate into their hearts, producing lasting changes that will bear much fruit. To God be the Glory! It pays to obey.

You may be preaching at the moment to a handful of people. What a privilege. What an awesome responsibility. Keep seeking the Lord for what He wants you to say to those precious sheep and one day the Lord Himself will increase the anointing upon you. Just keep being faithful. Don't try to run before you can walk. Trust the Lord to increase your ministry as He directs. Never try to promote yourself. It is far better to grow gently, one step at a time. Many have found themselves too deep too quickly and become shipwrecked. Take all the stages as if you were climbing up a ladder. One rung at a time. That is the sure way.

This verse is so true for those in ministry:

> *'A man's gift maketh room for him, and bringeth him before great men.'*   (Proverbs 18:16)

I have sat through meetings over the years and listened to some people from a Christian platform, and then left the meeting wondering if they were ever called to preach in the first place. Without a definite call from God there can never be an anointing to preach. Make sure that you are called of God in the first place before you start preaching. This is the responsibility of the local church to give people opportunity in the pulpit to see if there is any evidence of the anointing. We do this all the time in our church. Every so often we give someone new a chance to prepare a ten-minute message. This way we can assess whether or not that person has a gift, or **not**. There are also those who want to preach all the time. Such people have to be held back for their sake and everybody else's!

We shall deal with the issue of increasing the anointing upon our preaching in a later chapter.

Obedience to the General Will of God

The general will of God for our lives is found in the written Word of God: the Bible. As you read through its pages the Holy Spirit will highlight areas of your life that need to change. Every time you see something that you should be doing and you start to do it, you have grown in the anointing. Simple obedience to the written Word of God will steadily increase the overall anointing upon you as a person. Also, if you see something through the Word and you ignore it then you will be holding back the anointing. It is far better to obey. It is so interesting how loving and caring our Father is regarding personal obedience. He will first of all speak through His Word and if we do not respond He will arrange for someone to preach on that very subject next Sunday – providing of course that they obey the Holy Spirit! The Lord is so patient with us and is often painstakingly thorough in getting the message through to us.

What happens if we still don't obey? That is a good question. If the Lord is convicting us of something that He wants removing from our lives then He will get our attention one way or another. I am amazed at how patient He is with us. He never gives up either. He is determined that we will grow in the anointing and get rid of those things that hinder it.

Many want to hear the Lord speak to them about their ministry etc. However, the specific will of God is not going to be revealed until we are obeying the general will of God. It is true that God does not wait until we are perfect in every detail before He calls us. If that were the case then nobody would be ministering. However, the Lord knows our hearts. I have often said to people who are embarking on leadership, 'The Lord doesn't call us for **who** we are but for **what we can become in Christ!**'

Obedience is so important in every area of life. Often the Lord will challenge us to give something up that displeases Him. I used to smoke cigarettes and knew that I had to give it up. I had been a Christian for about a year and was still hooked on tobacco. I had tried a couple of times to give up but not seriously enough. I knew that I could not go on with the Lord without giving up this habitual bondage. I found out who I was in Christ and was able to take authority over it myself. I was delivered overnight. I did it with all my heart because I did not want to delay the next stage of anointing in my life. I have never looked back. All sorts of things started to happen shortly afterwards and I have never wanted one since.

Sir Walter Raleigh has a lot to answer for! If only he had known how many lives would be destroyed by that stupid weed. If you are still smoking then let me spell out some things to help to motivate you to quit. Smoking is a slow suicide. Not only can it reduce your life expectancy and lead to several deadly diseases, but it also affects others around you. Those that you love are greatly affected by your nicotine addiction. Satan hates your guts and wants to remove you by any means he can. Smoking is already doing a good job to eliminate you from the battle. Another thing about smoking is that it is a terrible witness to others. Every time you try to share your faith with someone a little voice says, 'They can smell the smoke on you and think you are a lousy testimony.' They are right! Even if every other part of your life is right you jeopardise someone else's chance of accepting the love of God into their lives just because you are still smoking. Give it up! Make a quality decision right now to quit.

This goes for any other outward habit that needs to go. We have all authority over alcohol abuse, drugs or anything that stands in the way of our spiritual growth.

Once we are under way obeying the general will of God in His precious Word then we can enter the next exciting stage.

The Specific Will of God

This stage is only open to the following people!

1. Those Christians (truly born again) who are totally surrendered to the Lord.

2. Those who are true disciples of Christ by being fully committed to their local church.

3. Those who are submitted to the leadership of that church.

4. Those who are seeking to obey the written Word of God.

5. Those who repent and change. The sooner you repent the faster you are promoted.

6. Those who are baptised in water and the Holy Spirit and who give tithes and offerings to their local church. The windows of heaven are open upon those who tithe!

If The Holy Spirit reveals anything else to you personally then obey Him.

Now you can start to hear the specific will of your Father.

This is where a different level of anointing is released into our lives. The rest is building a foundation of obedience and being faithful in little. Now the real responsibility begins!

Remember that the Lord demands obedience. If you want to move forward then you have to obey His instructions. You will soon experience an anointing like nothing else as you step out on these commands from the Father.

My First Specific Instructions

Many years ago I was in a minister's meeting and I heard a voice telling me to give £5 to a colleague. I was quite shocked because I had never experienced His voice so clearly before. I looked into my wallet and saw two five pound notes and I prayed and said: 'Lord I only have £10 for the shopping this weekend for four Newports.' It was very definitely the voice of the Lord and so I handed John one of my five pound notes. He began to cry and told me that he had no money at all for his family! I was thrilled to have obeyed something so seemingly simple. That is not the end of the story because when I arrived home I was supposed to take Ruth to the shops along with our two babies. Within one hour of giving the £5 I opened the mail at home and there was £100 in an envelope! Twenty times what I had given. We did some shopping that day I can tell you!

Over the years I have learned to obey this specific voice of God and the responsibility has increased more and more.

One day in Manchester while I was pastoring a church there the Lord told me to lead the people in dancing. Many of the church wanted to dance as part of worship but I was still too religious and **English**. I thought that dancing was not for an Englishman. Anyway I tried dancing in the lounge at home and in my office at church. But I flatly refused to dance in public. Enough is enough ... I thought.

The months passed by and I still did not dance. Then I developed an open sore in my hand which would not heal. I rebuked it and confessed the Word but it got worse. I even used cream but that did not help. It was so painful that it got my attention. I was about to learn a very serious lesson about the specific will of God. Once His Word has been given to you there is no backing out. He demands a response.

I was at a conference and my hand was hurting so much. It was now stinging constantly and had been for six months. I spent some time in prayer and the Lord spoke to me and told me that I was in rebellion! I was stunned! **Me**, Lord?! He then told me that He had told me to dance two years ago and I still had not obeyed! I said that I did not think that it was that important and then I had an amazing revelation! Everything that the Lord says to you is important. Even dancing in my case. I can hear you laughing again at my expense – or is it yours!

I repented and told the Lord that I would dance on Sunday morning in front of everyone.

However, we had a three-week crusade booked with an evangelist that started on the Sunday morning. The church was packed and I had to repent publicly in front of them all. I asked the church to forgive me and they did and told me to get on with the service. I asked the praise team to lead a lively chorus and I danced in front of everyone, expecting them all to join me. I was the only one dancing – the rotten lot! God had promised me that my hand would be healed in a week. By the Friday it was totally healed. I have never had it since.

This was such a lesson for me to learn. Anyway, the whole church (well most of them anyway!) began dancing and we had a revival of signs and wonders! I am no longer an Englishman. I am a citizen of heaven. I have been in services all over the world and been led by the Lord to get them all dancing and get rid of that religious spirit. Dancing is one of the best ways of doing that.

'If ye be willing and obedient, ye shall eat the good of the land: But if ye refuse and rebel, ye shall be devoured with the sword: for the mouth of the LORD hath spoken it.'   (Isaiah 1:19–20)

'And Samuel said, Hath the LORD as great delight in burnt offerings and sacrifices, as in obeying the voice of the LORD? Behold, to obey is better than sacrifice, and to hearken than the fat of rams. For rebellion is as the sin of witchcraft, and stubbornness is as iniquity and idolatry. Because thou hast rejected the word of the LORD, he hath also rejected thee from being king.'

(1 Samuel 15:22–23)

This is very serious! Every time we rebel against the spoken Word of God it is treated as witchcraft! Make a serious quality decision to **obey every time He speaks**, and to eliminate all rebellion and see the anointing grow much quicker in your life.

'Why dost thou strive against him? for he giveth not account of any of his matters. For God speaketh once, yea twice, yet man perceiveth it not. In a dream, in a vision of the night, when deep sleep falleth upon men, in slumberings upon the bed; Then he openeth the ears of men, and sealeth their instruction, That he may withdraw man from his purpose, and hide pride from man.'   (Job 33:13–17)

Only the things that God has initiated will bear fruit on the Earth. You and I can do nothing on our own.

'Abide in me, and I in you. As the branch cannot bear fruit of itself, except it abide in the vine; no more can ye, except ye abide in me. I am the vine, ye are the branches: He that abideth in me, and I in him, the same bringeth forth much fruit: for without me ye can do nothing. If a man abide not in me, he is cast forth as a branch, and is withered; and men gather them, and cast them into the fire, and they are burned.'

(John 15:4–6)

Chapter 9

The Square Bashing is Over!

I hope you understand the title! For those who may not, let me explain. Every new army recruit, when he first arrives, has to learn discipline by doing mundane and often tiresome routines. But marching up and down with a rifle and full kit for weeks at a time seems pointless! Going on assault courses and using dummies instead of a real enemy must be an anticlimax. However, **this kind of training is absolutely vital** in any army.

One of the things that you have to learn in the army is **speedy obedience** to your commanding officer. Out on a real mission this can be the difference between life and death for you and others! These things have to be learnt where there is no responsibility involved.

So it is in God's army. We are all in preparation and training for the real thing. Sometimes in the natural army they have to go on special training for specific tasks. The same is true in the kingdom of God. That is why we need to learn quickly because you never know what the Lord is training you for next. The army is rarely told about their mission until they are in the middle of it. I have found the same to be true about the work of the Lord. I have often felt myself being trained for something and only realised afterwards what was going on.

The reason I am saying all of this is all to do with the anointing. In the last five years the Lord has taken me completely by surprise in the things that He has called upon me to do. I am doing things now that I never dreamed I would be doing.

I remember praying one day many years ago something like this: 'Lord, you are not getting much by having me in your service but one thing I will give you is this; I will go anywhere you send me, do anything that you tell me and say anything you want me to.' He has kept me to that prayer many times!

One thing I never wanted to do was to go to America. That was the first place He told me to go to. I hopped on a plane to California with very little money in my pocket and trusted the Lord for everything. What was I doing? The devil told me I was stupid. I agreed with him! I felt daft. However, the Lord had told me to go and I obeyed Him. Miracle after miracle took place and He looked after me so well. I arrived back from that trip thinking that the Lord was just seeing if I would obey Him. I have since been to 35 countries in five years and He keeps sending me to new places. I have recently been commanded to go to Iceland, Beijing and Shanghai as part of the call on my life to do territorial warfare. I have taken teams from our church to places like Israel, Sri Lanka, Nepal and Europe.

Another task in my life that I never wanted to do was to write books. This is my twelfth book in six years! Someone once said that the pen was mightier than the sword. I have been amazed at how many people have read my books. To our knowledge we currently have books in about 40 countries! Some have been translated into different languages also. One of our books was recently used at a pastor's conference in Japan to discuss the five-fold ministry gifts. Another book was sent to Cambodia where it was translated and is now used to train leaders in a Pentecostal Bible College. We have just had a letter from Alaska from a lady who had just read one of our books and wanted more information. I once had a telephone call from Jamaica asking for our books after someone had read about us. I received a fax recently from Southern Australia asking for permission to use my material in a new Christian magazine! And so it goes on.

Zechariah 4:10a says:

'For who hath despised the day of small things?'

If we are faithful in the little tasks that the Father places before us then He will promote us to higher and higher realms for His Glory. In fact, I believe that every time He tells us to do something He is actually watching us to see if He can use us in a bigger way. Sometimes He gives us a taste of the next stage in our life and sees how we cope with it! If there is a hint of pride, ego or arrogance then we usually have to deal with it somehow!

The Lord spoke to me recently about His call on my life that quite took me aback. He said this to me: 'I am more determined to see the call I have placed on your life fulfilled than you are.' That word has shaken the slack out of me I can assure you. I now want to be as determined as my Father to see His call fulfilled through me by staying humble before Him, seeking His face and obeying His every command. This ensures that the anointing **reaches its maximum**. Too many people go through life hardly producing anything of lasting value. I trust that this little book will challenge you to seek a fruitful life and reach the high calling of God upon your life. It is available for everyone. Not just a few.

Jesus Christ is the Holy and Anointed One inside of you who longs to show Himself through you in all His wonderful majesty. We are all called to do something different in the body of Christ which is unique. It is your job to find out what that is and to do it with all you have got!

So many people are waiting for the Lord to use them thinking that they are waiting for God. He is waiting for **you**. Be faithful in little. Submit to your local leadership. Be super generous in financial giving to your local church. Seek the face of God like never before. Then start to expect a new wave of anointing in your own personal life as you obey each thing that the Father brings across your path.

The Biggest Promotion in My Life

I always knew that there was more to the Christian life than what I was experiencing. Then one day I read a book about a man who saw into the spirit realm. He could actually see angels, demons and the Lord Himself. This challenged me to ask the Father if I could one day see like that. Ten years later I had an attack on my life that nearly killed me. I almost died in a head-on car crash doing 70 miles an hour. The enemy tried all he could to destroy me at that time in my life, but he failed! However, as I came out of that major assault on my life and ministry the most amazing thing started to happen. I actually saw the evil spirit that was assigned to me. Since that day I have seen into the spirit realm on numerous occasions. I have had angels to come up to me and talk to me. I have watched angels engage in spiritual warfare. I have had demons come and fight with me! I have even had the Lord Jesus Christ Himself visit me and talk to me. I do not say that lightly. In fact every time I mention it I can sense the awesomeness of that experience. I will never be the same after that experience. I will share it with you now for I believe a new anointing came upon me from that day that is very special to me.

We were having our prayer meeting before our deliverance school as we always do. Suddenly as we were praying, all eight of us were overcome by the power of the Holy Spirit. I had only ever experienced this once before as strongly. None of us were able to move. I tried to move my arms but could not. All I could move were my eyes! Nobody could speak either. Then I saw a group of angels come down from heaven with Jesus in the middle. They were all smiling and laughing together. As they walked down our corridor I noticed that there were in fact three angels plus Jesus Christ the Anointed One!

The three angels stood outside the door and only the Lord Jesus Christ came into our prayer room. I watched Him come straight up to me and He slapped me heartily on my shoulder in a very friendly, brotherly way, and said this: 'Hi Trev, it's your brother Jesus here. I've just come to tell you that your ministry is about to start.' He smiled with such a wide, beaming smile and walked out of the room. I then watched Him go up towards heaven with the three angels and disappear. We were all under the anointing for about five more minutes before it lifted and we were able to move.

I am just starting to realise what that visitation means after three years. I should perhaps mention that the Lord had been telling me for three years previously to accept the call as an apostle. I made sure that it was definitely of God before accepting it. This visit from Jesus came about two weeks after I had accepted the apostolic call. I never wanted to be called an apostle and would never have called myself one. I am still plain old Trevor Newport with all his weaknesses and frailty. But there is an anointing upon my life that has been initiated from heaven itself to fulfil a purpose on the earth which I am determined to see come to pass. I often feel that I am just beginning as His will unfolds in stages. In fact, the larger our ministry gets, the smaller I feel and that is a very healthy attitude!

The following scriptures have always been a challenge to me:

> *'(Now the man Moses was very meek, above all the men which were upon the face of the earth.) And the LORD spake suddenly unto Moses, and unto Aaron, and unto Miriam, Come out ye three unto the tabernacle of the congregation. And they three came out. And the LORD came down in the pillar of the cloud, and stood in the door of the tabernacle, and called Aaron and Miriam: and they both came forth. And he said, Hear now my words: If there be a prophet among you, I the LORD will make myself known unto him in a vision, and will speak unto him in a dream. My servant Moses is not so, who is faithful in all mine house. With him will I speak mouth to mouth, even apparently, and not in dark speeches; and the similitude of the LORD shall he behold: wherefore then were ye not afraid to speak against my servant Moses?'*   (Numbers 12:3–8)

There is nothing wrong with dreams and visions. That is one of the ways that the Lord communicates with His people. But this passage tells us that there is something higher than dreams and visions. That is the direct voice of the Lord. I have always wanted that! This is the highest level of relationship with our heavenly Father. He talks to me about all sorts of things. I talk to Him about all kinds of things as well both in the spiritual world and in the natural. My desire is to live in the Throne Room at all times. There is no warfare there. Sometimes there is a battle to get into the Throne

Room but once you are there it is just intimacy with the Father and His Son Jesus Christ. That is where I get all my instructions from to lead Life-Changing Ministries. The passage below reveals something else about those who are anointed to hear from the Lord. Don't speak against them.

1 Chronicles 16:22 says:

> *'Saying, **Touch not mine anointed, and do my prophets no harm.'***

The Lord is the avenger of all who touch His faithful servants. Be warned!

Chapter 10

How to Increase the Anointing

There are things that can either cause the anointing upon our lives to diminish or increase. We need to identify the areas that cause the anointing to diminish and to eliminate them. Also we need to implement all the ways that cause the anointing to grow. This is so simple and yet so many people get caught up in things which slow down their effectiveness. The devil is still the most subtle of all the created beings. He knows his job. Never underestimate him. He is constantly on the lookout for a chance to slow us down or put us out of the game completely.

We are now going to look through some areas of life to see if there are any changes to be made. Remember that this is a positive exercise to see all the negative footholds of the enemy replaced by the anointing. This is probably the most significant part of this book to help you to grow in the anointing so don't skip this part! Resist the devil right now.

Telling Lies

> 'He that worketh deceit shall not dwell within my house: he that telleth lies shall not tarry in my sight.'
>
> (Psalm 101:7)

> *'But speaking the truth in love, may grow up into him in all things, which is the head, even Christ.'*
>
> (Ephesians 4:15)

Criticism

> *'Judge not, that ye be not judged.'* (Matthew 7:1)

A critical spirit needs to be repented of because it will ultimately destroy all the anointing in you. Develop a gentle, loving spirit. The anointing of the Holy Spirit is definitely not attracted to a critical spirit.

Moaning and Complaining

> *'And when the people complained, it displeased the LORD: and the LORD heard it; and his anger was kindled; and the fire of the LORD burnt among them, and consumed them that were in the uttermost parts of the camp.'*
>
> (Numbers 11:1)

> *'These are murmurers, complainers, walking after their own lusts; and their mouth speaketh great swelling words, having men's persons in admiration because of advantage.'*
>
> (Jude 1:16)

> *'Do all things without murmurings and disputings.'*
>
> (Philippians 2:14)

The anointing of the Spirit is quickly removed from all those who gripe, moan or complain, so watch for these missiles and repent if you have fallen into these sins.

Gossiping

> *'But shun profane and vain babblings: for they will increase unto more ungodliness. And their word will eat as doth a canker: of whom is Hymenaeus and Philetus.'*
>
> (2 Timothy 2:16–17)

> *'To speak evil of no man, to be no brawlers, but gentle, shewing all meekness unto all men.'* (Titus 3:2)

We all need to be aware of these things at all times. These are things which can speedily erode the precious anointing of the Spirit upon our lives.

Staying away from the House of the Lord

Imagine a nice coal fire in the winter time. The coals are burning brightly as they are all together in that miniature inferno. If you remove one of the burning coals and place it on the hearth you will notice two things; firstly, the fire stays the same and keeps on burning and secondly the one coal removed goes out very quickly! So it is with those who stay away from God's house. The flame soon goes out without you noticing. Others can tell that the flame is going out but you cannot. That is one of the devil's lies. Look at what the Word says:

> *'Not forsaking the assembling of ourselves together, as the manner of some is; but exhorting one another: and so much the more, as ye see the day approaching.'*
>
> (Hebrews 10:25)

> *'Abide in me, and I in you. As the branch cannot bear fruit of itself, except it abide in the vine; no more can ye, except ye abide in me.'* (John 15:4)

I urge you in these last days not to get distracted from the main priorities in life. Going to the House of the Lord must stay right at the top in your list of priorities.

The enemy loves to tempt some people away from church for seemingly legitimate reasons, but I would say that virtually anything that takes you away from the house of God is from the evil one to seek to remove the anointing from your life. Remember that nobody 'plans' to backslide. It comes in very subtly. Watch out. Nobody is immune from Satan's tactics.

Unforgiveness, Resentment, Bitterness and Hate

I have written a small booklet entitled *The Two U's* which deals with unbelief and unforgiveness. I believe that these two forces are probably the most powerful missiles used by the enemy against Christians. In my pastoral responsibilities over the years I have had to deal with hundreds of people and the things that stop the full flow of the Holy Spirit are these two areas again and again.

'So likewise shall my heavenly Father do also unto you, if ye from your hearts forgive not every one his brother their trespasses.'   (Matthew 18:35)

'For if ye forgive men their trespasses, your heavenly Father will also forgive you: But if ye forgive not men their trespasses, neither will your Father forgive your trespasses.'   (Matthew 6:14–15)

'Let all bitterness, and wrath, and anger, and clamour, and evil speaking, be put away from you, with all malice: And be ye kind one to another, tenderhearted, forgiving one another, even as God for Christ's sake hath forgiven you.'   (Ephesians 4:31, 32)

'Looking diligently lest any man fail of the grace of God; lest any root of bitterness springing up trouble you, and thereby many be defiled.'   (Hebrews 12:15)

I have been saddened by the number of Christians who do not let go of past hurts. Forgive and forget! It is that simple. You are not going to go any further in the anointing if these things are not dealt with. The devil is laughing at such people who think that they can move forward while still holding onto unforgiveness. **Get rid of it today!** Forgive that person right now and renounce and repent of all resentment, bitterness and hate. A fresh anointing will come upon you enabling you to advance in the Kingdom.

As you read through the New Testament just make a note at how many times Jesus makes mention of forgiveness. Here is another example:

'Therefore I say unto you, What things soever ye desire, when ye pray, believe that ye receive them, and ye shall have them. And when ye stand praying, forgive, if ye have ought against any: that your Father also which is in heaven may forgive you your trespasses. But if ye do not forgive, neither will your Father which is in heaven forgive your trespasses.'

(Mark 11:24–26)

Thus we cannot get our prayers answered if we do not forgive. The anointing is therefore greatly affected by unforgiveness! If there is someone who you still struggle with then speak that person's name out loud right now and forgive them. Then rebuke the devil and resist him and all forms of resentment etc.

Unbelief!

> *'Take heed, brethren, lest there be in any of you an evil heart of unbelief, in departing from the living God.'*
>
> (Hebrews 3:12)

Read the whole chapter of Hebrews 3.

If your mother or father told you something then you would usually believe them. They would not be very pleased with you if you did not believe them. How much more if we do not believe the creator of the universe, The King of kings and Lord of lords when He tells us something and we do not believe it. This is unbelief and will diminish the anointing on your life faster than anything else. Repent of all unbelief right now out loud and resist this sinister force. Mention before the Lord any area that you struggle to believe Him in, and ask for forgiveness from unbelief in that area. Then faith can come which brings the anointing.

> *'But without faith it is impossible to please him: for he that cometh to God must believe that he is, and that he is a rewarder of them that diligently seek him.'*
>
> (Hebrews 11:6)

Guard your life in all areas regarding unbelief because the anointing of the Holy Spirit will not flow in an area which causes defeat, sadness and misery. So many people have victory in some areas, but not in all. Write down any areas where you are defeated, attack the unbelief with faith and start to see a change for the better. Some people have faith in every area apart from one which needs to be addressed. Many have faith in all areas of life apart from their marriage. Don't let unbelief in that area of life rob you of having heaven on earth with your partner. Speak faith now into your marriage and repent of speaking against your partner for life. If you have no anointing in your marriage then it will affect all the other areas of your ministry. Attend to your marriage if you are married. If you are single then you will have other areas that need attention. Incidentally, if you are single and think that getting married will be the answer to all your problems then think again. Don't be naive. For many it is the most challenging area of life. One preacher once said, 'marriage doesn't work! You have to work at marriage.' I would certainly agree with that. It takes patience, hard work, forgiveness, longsuffering, gentleness and a lot of faith to see heaven on earth with your spouse! Ruth and I have both had to work hard at our marriage because of the many differences between us. We love each other very much but when two people are so close they can often clash. This is where the ultimate test for a Christian comes into being. The Lord knew what He was doing when He established marriage. I am shortly going to write a book about 'The Family' which will include all relationships within the family.

Negative Talking

'Death and life are in the power of the tongue: and they that love it shall eat the fruit thereof.' (Proverbs 18:21)

'O generation of vipers, how can ye, being evil, speak good things? for out of the abundance of the heart the mouth speaketh.' (Matthew 12:34)

Our words carry awesome power! We need to watch what we say about everything. This will protect the anointing upon our lives for good. I really believe that. Jesus said:

'For verily I say unto you, That whosoever shall say unto this mountain, Be thou removed, and be thou cast into the sea; and shall not doubt in his heart, but shall believe that those things which he saith shall come to pass; he shall have whatsoever he saith.' (Mark 11:23)

Jesus Christ said this! Once I had understood this verse of Scripture I went to work on my vocabulary! All the things that were against the Word of God I sought to eliminate from my speech. I removed things about death, fear, sickness, poverty, lack, or anything negative. I took Jesus at His word and the peace that came into my life was awesome. I speak positively about everything. If I realise that I am speaking negatively about something then I do some work on my confession.

Your words will either create or destroy, help or hinder, bind or heal. I often say from the pulpit, 'If you haven't got anything good to say ... keep quiet!'

Pride, Ego and Selfish Ambition

> *'The fear of the LORD is to hate evil: pride, and arrogancy, and the evil way, and the froward mouth, do I hate.'*   (Proverbs 8:13)

> *'When pride cometh, then cometh shame: but with the lowly is wisdom.'*   (Proverbs 11:2)

> *'But he giveth more grace. Wherefore he saith, **God resisteth the proud, but giveth grace unto the humble.**'*
>   (James 4:6)

Some people think that this means they cannot take pride in their appearance or pride in their work and must do everything in a shoddy manner. How foolish we are. This is not what pride means at all. Others think that to be humble means to be poor and to be rich is proud. This is not true at all. I know some rich people and they are very humble and I know some poor people and they are full of pride!

The Strong's dictionary gives the definition of proud as *huperephanos*: appearing above others (conspicuous), i.e. (figuratively) haughty.

This would certainly be true regarding the Pharisees who saw themselves above others. No wonder Jesus was so hard on them. This kind of pride will remove any anointing from our lives and cause all kinds of forces to attack us. True humility continues to seek God, stays in the Word, acknowledges God in everything and gives God all the Glory! A wrong understanding of humility will produce a poor self image and not be glorifying to the Lord.

Those in ministry have to guard against pride when success begins to happen in their work. However, success in ministry does not mean that you have to be proud. Some of the humblest people lead the greatest works. Every wise minister should recognise that it is only the quality of those people who are working with him (or her) that helps to produce a strong work.

Thus as we keep humble in our ministries the anointing can increase more and more and never stop growing until Jesus returns. This should surely be our goal.

Wrong Relationships

'Be not deceived: evil communications corrupt good manners.'   (1 Corinthians 15:33)

The people that you associate with will either help your anointing to grow or help you to lose it! Some will take you away from the Lord and some will encourage you to be closer to Him. Some will appear fine to start with but then take you away after a while. Satan uses wolves in sheep's clothing to deceive many. Be careful who you associate with. The closer you are to the anointing of the Spirit the less likely you are to fall into silly traps. It is when people are away from the Spirit of God that they start to associate with the wrong kind and once a friendship has started it is difficult to stop. Your entire relationship with God Almighty will be affected for better or worse by everyone that you befriend. Therefore be on your guard at all times in the area of friendships. If someone is influencing you in the wrong way then **say something** and seek to lead them back to God. If they will not respond then **part company with them**! There are plenty more friends who will do you good instead of harm. Don't be gullible or naive in this area. Your whole future depends on it!

Sin

'If I regard iniquity in my heart, the Lord will not hear me.'   (Psalm 66:18)

This seems very obvious I know, but someone could read this right now and repent of sin and receive a new anointing into their lives. Sin separates us from the anointing.

> *'If we confess our sins, he is faithful and just to forgive*
> *us our sins, and to cleanse us from all unrighteousness.'*
> (1 John 1:9)

Don't wait until you are convicted before you repent. As soon as you realise that you have sinned then repent. We do this by confessing the sin and asking for forgiveness. The blood of Jesus then cleanses us and we should be stronger against that particular sin the next time.

> *'For sin shall not have dominion over you: for ye are not under*
> *the law, but under grace.'*   (Romans 6:14)

Sin does not have authority over us but we have authority over sin!

> *'And the times of this ignorance God winked at; **but now***
> ***commandeth all men every where to repent.'***
> (Acts 17:30)

Keep short accounts with God and don't let any subtle sins into your life. It has been said by many that whatever sins we were involved in before we came to know Jesus Christ as Saviour are the areas that each individual needs to be especially careful of. For the person who was an alcoholic (or heading that way) then he needs to be always on his guard against alcohol. It does not seem to bother some Christians to have a glass of wine from time to time with a meal. However, others don't stop at just one glass! That is an area of weakness for some and so total abstinence is strongly recommended. I should know because that is what I came out of. I have been in cultural situations where all the Christians drink wine with their meal and it does not affect them.

What sins were you involved in before conversion? Make sure that none of them creep back into your life in moments of weakness. We have power over them all through the blood of Jesus Christ! Don't give the devil a foothold by falling into blatant sin.

> ***'Neither give place to the devil.'***   (Ephesians 4:27)

> *'Wherefore seeing we also are compassed about with so great*
> *a cloud of witnesses, **let us lay aside every weight, and the***

sin which doth so easily beset us, and let us run with patience the race that is set before us.'   (Hebrews 12:1)

Sport, Hobbies, Pastimes and Relaxation

We all need something to help us to shut off from work etc. Some like one thing and another enjoys something else. I enjoy playing golf once in a while, or table-tennis with my son. My wife enjoys swimming and, as a family, we watch a movie from time to time. None of these are wrong provided that we are in control of them and not the other way around. Some people get addicted to television and watch all day long or several hours every night. If anything will reduce the anointing upon our lives then TV will! We all need to be disciplined in this area of life. It can become an idol like anything else which will stop the flow of the anointing through us. This is another area where I have to be careful because I watched far too much as a child and it became a habit. That is one of the reasons that we did not have a TV in our home for 10 years. We concentrated on the ministry and raising our children by giving a lot of parental attention. Vision is extremely powerful and so we need to be careful what we put into our minds. Children are especially vulnerable. I have been shocked at how much occult content is included in many children's programmes. Don't bring your children up with square eyes.

> *'For bodily exercise profiteth little: but godliness is profitable unto all things, having promise of the life that now is, and of that which is to come.'*   (1 Timothy 4:8)

> *'And what agreement hath the temple of God with idols? for ye are the temple of the living God; as God hath said, I will dwell in them, and walk in them; and I will be their God, and they shall be my people.'*   (2 Corinthians 6:16)

> *'Little children, keep yourselves from idols. Amen.'*
> (1 John 5:21)

> *'Thou shalt have no other gods before me.'*
> (Exodus 20:3)

If you have anything in your life that would be classed as an idol because it comes before your devotion to the Lord then repent right now and have a fresh release of the anointing in your life. Look through this check list and see if any of these things comes before God.

1. You!
2. Your job.
3. Money.
4. Possessions.
5. Your family! (God first, family second, ministry third.)
6. Hobbies.
7. TV.
8. Your ministry!
9. Your status in life.
10. . . . . (put anything else that you know of).

Chapter 11

Things Which Cause
the Anointing to Accelerate

Fasting and Prayer

We have already determined that our Father deposits an anointing into our lives at the new birth (when we are born again) but He then gives us things to do to cause that anointing to grow.

Fasting helps us to move out of the flesh and into the spiritual realm much faster than anything else. Notice what Jesus did at the start of His earthly ministry:

> *'And when he had fasted forty days and forty nights, he was afterward an hungred.'* (Matthew 4:2)

He began with a fast to prepare Him for three-and-a-half years of intense work.

> *'Is it such a fast that I have chosen? a day for a man to afflict his soul? is it to bow down his head as a bulrush, and to spread sackcloth and ashes under him? wilt thou call this a fast, and an acceptable day to the LORD? Is not this the fast that I have chosen? To loose the bands of wickedness, to undo the heavy burdens, and to let the oppressed go free, and that ye break every yoke? Is it not to deal thy bread to the hungry, and that thou bring the poor that are cast out to thy house? When thou seest the naked, that thou cover him; and that thou hide not thyself from thine own flesh? **Then shall thy***

> *light break forth as the morning, and thine health shall spring forth speedily: and thy righteousness shall go before thee; the glory of the* LORD *shall be thy reward.'*
>
> (Isaiah 58:5–8)

Read the whole chapter and just see what the rewards are for fasting before the Lord. A breakthrough in the anointing is assured.

For the first twelve years of ministry I gave myself to fasting regularly every week. I would fast at least two days each week and sometimes three days with just liquids. My body became so used to fasting that after a while it would expect to go without food for a season. I still fast every week but do not keep to the same sort of routine since my life has changed so much from being a pastor to an apostle with an extremely varied life. No two weeks are ever the same whereas when I was 'just' pastoring I could have more routine.

Praying in the Spirit

I have written a booklet on praying in the Holy Spirit which can be ordered from the address at the back. Basically, when you pray in tongues you start to open up the spiritual dimension. As you continue praying in tongues you enter different stages of the anointing and eventually you reach the Throne Room where there is no opposition from the enemy. This should be every believer's goal. Order the booklet and study it and your prayer life will never be boring again. Prayer is two-way communication with the Father. It is not just you talking to Him, but the Father speaking to you as well.

Praying and fasting helps us to tune our spirit in with the Holy Spirit of God which causes the anointing upon our lives to grow more and more.

> *'As they ministered to the Lord, and fasted, the Holy Ghost said, Separate me Barnabas and Saul for the work whereunto I have called them. And when they had fasted and prayed, and laid their hands on them, they sent them away.'*
>
> (Acts 13:2–3)

The Written Word of God

I know that I have already mentioned this in an earlier chapter but it is relevant here also. In fact, reading the Bible is relevant all the time. None of us reads the Word of God enough!

> *'For the word of God is quick, and powerful, and sharper than any two-edged sword, piercing even to the dividing asunder of soul and spirit, and of the joints and marrow, and is a discerner of the thoughts and intents of the heart.'*
>
> (Hebrews 4:12)

> *'All Scripture is given by inspiration of God, and is profitable for doctrine, for reproof, for correction, for instruction in righteousness.'*   (2 Timothy 3:16)

Spend quality time every day soaking up the Word of God and see the anointing released upon your life.

A Lifestyle of Praise

> *'And at midnight **Paul and Silas prayed, and sang praises unto God**: and the prisoners heard them. **And suddenly there was a great earthquake**, so that the foundations of the prison were shaken: and immediately all the doors were opened, and every one's bands were loosed.'*
>
> (Acts 16:25–26)

What an anointing upon praise to God.

> *'By him therefore let us offer the sacrifice of praise to God continually, that is, the fruit of our lips giving thanks to his name.'*   (Hebrews 13:15)

> *'**I will bless the** LORD **at all times: his praise shall continually be in my mouth.**'*   (Psalm 34:1)

This is so powerful for every believer because if you are constantly praising, then you are in a very positive mode at all times. It is difficult to sin, gripe, moan, complain, be afraid, worry, murmur or do anything negative if you are praising the Lord! When I am driving I usually listen to praise music all the time. It is good use of time and it helps me to focus on magnifying God all the time.

> *'Rejoice in the Lord, ye righteous; and give thanks at the remembrance of his holiness.'* (Psalm 97:12)

> *'Let them shout for joy, and be glad, that favour my righteous cause: yea, let them say continually, Let the Lord be magnified, which hath pleasure in the prosperity of his servant.'* (Psalm 35:27)

> *'Then he said unto them, Go your way, eat the fat, and drink the sweet, and send portions unto them for whom nothing is prepared: for this day is holy unto our Lord: **neither be ye sorry; for the joy of the Lord is your strength.**'* (Nehemiah 8:10)

The devil is after our joy because if you lose your joy you lose your strength. Keep rejoicing and have a continual feast.

> *'All the days of the afflicted are evil: but he that is of a merry heart hath a continual feast.'* (Proverbs 15:15)

Be a Worshipper!

There is a big difference between praise and worship!

> *'But the hour cometh, and now is, when the true worshippers shall worship the Father in spirit and in truth: for the Father seeketh such to worship him.'* (John 4:23)

The Father is seeking true worshippers. Every so often as part of my devotion to the Lord I will sit quietly before Him and use a video of my favourite worship and just worship the Father. I do this sometimes for hours at a time. I can feel the anointing of His presence all over me and it is wonderful.

> *'Give unto the Lord the glory due unto his name; worship the Lord in the beauty of holiness.'* (Psalm 29:2)

> *'O come, let us worship and bow down: let us kneel before the Lord our maker.'* (Psalm 95:6)

I find that in a service that if there is real release of true worship then the gifts of the Holy Spirit start to flow easily. I also find that corporate worship where everyone is together as one voice before the Lord releases an anointing of the Presence of the Holy Spirit like nothing else on Earth! When we were in Salford, Manchester, we had an awesome move of the Spirit which had its central focus on praise and worship. I would often leave the service and still be crying with His presence up to three hours after the meeting had finished. I have yet to be in meetings like that since.

Recently, in our church in Stoke-on-Trent we saw a whole row of angels join us for worship and I have seen them since. Worship is awesome. Make sure when you go to church that your heart is right with God and people and take church seriously! Don't just sit there like a stone and let everyone else worship. Join in with them and experience the wonder, awe, majesty and Divine Presence of the Almighty God and you will hunger for it more and more.

Therefore, if you want to increase in the anointing you must make a quality decision to seek His face continually and seek to dwell in His presence every day of your life.

'When thou saidst, Seek ye my face; my heart said unto thee,
Thy face, LORD, will I seek.' (Psalm 27:8)

Chapter 12

The Fruit of the Holy Spirit

Read the following scriptures carefully:

> *'This I say then, Walk in the Spirit, and ye shall not fulfil the lust of the flesh. For the flesh lusteth against the Spirit, and the Spirit against the flesh: and these are contrary the one to the other: so that ye cannot do the things that ye would. But if ye be led of the Spirit, ye are not under the law. Now the works of the flesh are manifest, which are these; Adultery, fornication, uncleanness, lasciviousness, idolatry, witchcraft, hatred, variance, emulations, wrath, strife, seditions, heresies, envyings, murders, drunkenness, revellings, and such like: of the which I tell you before, as I have also told you in time past, that they which do such things shall not inherit the kingdom of God. **But the fruit of the Spirit is love, joy, peace, longsuffering, gentleness, goodness, faith, meekness, temperance: against such there is no law.**'*
>
> (Galatians 5:16–23)

Life brings many challenges for the fruit of the Spirit! Every day we are confronted with opportunities to grow in the fruit or to operate in the flesh. Every time we operate in love rather than hate then the anointing upon us grows. When we are persecuted for righteousness' sake and we take it joyfully then we grow in that area of the anointing.

So it is with all aspects of the spiritual fruit.

> *'Ye shall know them by their fruits. Do men gather grapes of thorns, or figs of thistles?*
>
> (Matthew 7:16)

'Wherefore by their fruits ye shall know them.'
(Matthew 7:20)

The true acid test of a Christian is not the gifts of the Spirit but the fruit of the Spirit. We must be always developing in this area to grow up to full maturity in Christ Jesus.

Many people want a mighty anointing upon their ministries but never achieve this because of not growing up in the fruit. Patience is a vital quality to developing in the anointing. Joshua is heralded as a great spiritual leader but only after waiting many years as servant to Moses. Joseph had an awesome responsibility to fulfil but had to wait two decades before his dreams were realised. The anointing of the Holy Spirit grows as we are patient through trials, testings and temptations.

How are you developing in this area of your Christian growth? Make a list of the areas that you need to grow in. It is always a good exercise to write things down and then to pray about them.

Another of the fruits is meekness. Another word for this is humbleness.

*'Likewise, ye younger, submit yourselves unto the elder. Yea, all of you be subject one to another, and **be clothed with humility: for God resisteth the proud, and giveth grace to the humble.'*** (1 Peter 5:5)

One of the main reasons why many do not grow very much in their ministry and calling is because of pride, ego and selfish ambition. We need to continually guard against pride and walk in true biblical humility to reach our full potential. True humility realises that we are only servants of His instructions. We cannot initiate anything ourselves. We need to rely on the Lord for everything to remain humble before Him. As the Lord releases a greater anointing upon us for, say, healing then we must be on our guard against pride as we see greater manifestations of the miraculous power of God. Always give God the glory for what He does through you and you will continue to grow in the anointing in each area of life.

Are there any areas of your life where you are not growing? It could be that pride has crept in.

Satan himself fell from heaven because of pride and every time we fall into pride we are playing into the devil's hand. A fall is waiting for all who do not humble themselves before God.

> *'Pride goeth before destruction, and an haughty spirit before a fall.'*   (Proverbs 16:18)

You might be asking what has all this got to do with the anointing? It has everything to do with it! One of the main reasons why many are not growing as they think that they should is because of this very issue. You are waiting for God to do something and He is waiting for you to climb down off your self-made pedestal and walk in true humility. I challenge you to make a tape recording of all that comes out of your mouth and see how many times you make proud statements! You may be quite shocked. God resists the proud! Also, because the Lord knows exactly what is in our hearts, He does not want us to fall flat on our faces causing great embarrassment to ourselves and His wonderful kingdom. These are strong words but I see it all too often. I watch many potential preachers eager to get an audience and I often sit back and see how the Father gently deals with them regarding these issues. The Lord wants to see us succeeding and not failing at the first hurdle. This is why we have to grow in stages. Every so often God will give you a chance to move forward for a little time and then He examines our hearts to see what is really inside us.

I have often looked at great preachers who carry an awesome anointing and wonder what kind of cost it took to get to that place. Probably much persecution, trials, abuse, false accusation and rejection. We all have to grow through the refiner's fire to be purged of all kinds of wrong motives and attitudes. These things do matter and the sooner that we take them seriously, the quicker the anointing can come upon us in a greater measure.

The Gifts of the Holy Spirit

We need both the gifts and the fruit to be complete in our calling. You will be unbalanced in your Christian walk if you do not develop in both.

'But the manifestation of the Spirit is given to every man to profit withal. For to one is given by the Spirit the word of wisdom; to another the word of knowledge by the same Spirit; to another faith by the same Spirit; to another the gifts of healing by the same Spirit; to another the working of miracles; to another prophecy; to another discerning of spirits; to another divers kinds of tongues; to another the interpretation of tongues: But all these worketh that one and the selfsame Spirit, dividing to every man severally as he will.'

(1 Corinthians 12:7–11)

There are nine gifts of the Spirit. The anointing upon each of these gifts grows as we develop in the Lord. Never be satisfied with your present revelation of these precious gifts.

These nine gifts can be put into three groups of three.

1. **The vocal gifts:**
   - Prophecy.
   - Divers kinds of tongues.
   - Interpretation of tongues.

2. **The revelation gifts:**
   - A word of knowledge.
   - A word of wisdom.
   - Discerning of spirits.

3. **The power gifts:**
   - The gifts of healings.
   - Working of miracles.
   - The gift of faith.

Once you are born again and know Christ as your own personal Saviour then you need to be baptised in water by full immersion (Mark 16:16; Acts 2:41; 8:26–40). Then, you can receive the baptism of the Holy Spirit with the evidence of speaking in tongues (Acts 2:4; Mark 16:17). Every Christian has the capacity to speak in tongues since we all receive the Holy Spirit when we are born again, but often we need to be shown how – as in the New Testament (Acts 19:2–6, for example).

This process can be reversed. In other words, you can be baptised in the Holy Spirit before water baptism, which did happen in the Bible.

Once you have gone through these two milestones of Christian development you are now a candidate for these nine spiritual gifts. When I first found out about these gifts I immediately asked for all of them! Why beat about the bush? Paul the apostle was the chief of all sinners and he had all nine gifts so I simply wanted to follow Paul. I have had people tell me that we cannot have all nine gifts, which I totally refute. It took several years before all nine anointings had manifested in my life but sure enough, one by one they were released through me to help people.

I am now going to describe to you the different anointings that I have experienced for each of these gifts.

Prophecy

> *'Having then gifts differing according to the grace that is given to us, whether prophecy, **let us prophesy according to the proportion of faith**.'*   (Romans 12:6)

I remember the first time I was given a prophecy in a public meeting. My heart started to beat quickly, a burden came upon me deep in my spirit and then a message came into my mind. My heart was pounding so much to the point that I had to offload this word. After I had given the word I felt a tremendous peace come over me. I was so glad to get it off my chest. This happened the first few times I had to prophesy. However, after the first few messages I noticed that I was getting less and less words in my mind. I realised that the Lord was stretching my faith and I had to launch out on what I had and then the rest would follow. This is the reason why many begin to prophesy and then stop because they do not realise that God is wanting more faith from you to step into. As I would begin with what I had the rest of the prophecy would follow. Also I noticed that I would have less and less feelings than when I started. My heart did not beat as fast. After a few years of prophesying the feelings became less and less and so did the words! One day I was given just a couple of words with no feelings whatsoever and I knew that once I stepped out in faith the rest would follow. It did. Then, I remember being given only one word and then a command from the Lord saying: prophesy! I got up and as soon as I opened my mouth the words just flowed out. Finally, I was in a meeting with many hundreds of people and the Lord spoke to me and said: prophesy! I had nothing at all. I stood up and opened my mouth and spoke what He gave me. This is growing in the gift of prophecy!

There have been times when I have had a vision in a meeting which I have had to describe, which is another aspect of prophecy. This gift of prophecy is also used in the context of personal prophecy for individuals which I have been used in many times. I am always more careful with giving personal words for people and usually tell the person to seek for confirmation about what I am saying. Personal prophecy is not infallible! It needs to be judged by the one receiving it. I have had many people come to with a 'word from the Lord' and have to say that 95% of all words for me have been wrong, guesswork or from the devil. A very small percentage have been from the Lord. Therefore, I have learned to wait on personal words until I am sure myself. Please learn from this those of you who give endless words for people. You are not doing anybody any favours by abusing this gifting. Personal prophecy comes out of your spirit not your mind. I pray you will grow up in this respect.

The way that I check a personal prophecy is that as soon as I hear it I wait for a witness of the Spirit. I can tell someone straight away if it was from God or not. This is where I depend on the anointing very much. I would recommend this course of action every time someone gives you a 'word from the Lord'.

Divers Kinds of Tongues

> 'To another the working of miracles; to another prophecy; to another discerning of spirits; **to another divers kinds of tongues;** to another the interpretation of tongues.'
>
> (1 Corinthians 12:10)

It must be said that this spiritual gift is separate from the personal prayer and praise language that we receive when we are baptised in the Holy Spirit. I can speak in tongues whenever I want to but I can only give a message in tongues to a church when I am anointed to do so. This is so important. I have been in meetings where someone gets up and simply speaks in their ordinary prayer language and expects to get an interpretation. I can tell when it is not a 'divers kind of tongue'. I usually get a witness of the Holy Spirit when I am leading a meeting and someone delivers a proper message in tongues.

I actually began to interpret tongues before I had ever given a public utterance in tongues. I have often had a word that I thought was a prophecy and all of a sudden someone would give a message in tongues. That is my confirmation to give my interpretation at that moment.

Note that it takes less faith to give an interpretation than a prophecy. You are on your own with prophecy whereas a tongue and interpretation helps to give confidence. It also takes less faith to give a message in tongues than a prophecy because you do not have to discern the message in tongues but everyone gets the responsibility to judge a prophecy.

Thus, to give a message in tongues requires the least faith, then interpretation and then prophecy requires the most faith.

Whenever I have given a message in tongues it is **always in a different language than my usual tongues**. I have often seen a language in front of me in vision which I have simply read out loud. Other times I receive a different language momentarily and once I have given it I do not remember the language, unlike the many tongues that I speak in my prayer tongue.

> '*I would that ye all spake with tongues, but rather that ye prophesied: for greater is he that prophesieth than he that speaketh with tongues, except he interpret, that the church may receive edifying. Now, brethren, if I come unto you speaking with tongues, what shall I profit you, except I shall speak to you either by revelation, or by knowledge, or by prophesying, or by doctrine?*'   (1 Corinthians 14:5–6)

> '*Wherefore let him that speaketh in an unknown tongue pray that he may interpret. For if I pray in an unknown tongue, my spirit prayeth, but my understanding is unfruitful. What is it*

then? I will pray with the spirit, and I will pray with the understanding also: I will sing with the spirit, and I will sing with the understanding also.' (1 Corinthians 14:13–15)

As you are used in these three vocal gifts you will notice that the anointing develops upon you causing you to be more and more confident and bold to deliver the message. I will never forget when my wife Ruth was called into the five-fold giftings to pastor our church. It was so noticeable when Ruth gave prophecy after that time that the authority was many times stronger than ever before. When Ruth gives a prophecy the room usually trembles with the anointing. It is such a joy to watch her develop after being shy and reserved for so many years. Whenever I go abroad on a trip Ruth has often prophesied over me with an anointing that is tangible. There is such a witness of the Holy Spirit when she prophesies that I always look forward to hearing her.

I have seen the gift of prophecy develop in my own life over 18 years and sometimes I am called upon by the Lord to prophesy over many people in one service. I am in Texas at this moment and just yesterday I went into a church and did not get the chance to preach because the spirit of prophecy came upon me and I gave about 25 personal prophecies to all the leaders of this particular Hispanic church. They told me afterwards that every prophetic word was absolutely spot on and impacted many lives.

I have been called upon by the Lord to prophesy to all sorts of people including top preachers which I always tremble a bit over.

The Lord sent me to speak a prophetic word over Russia for just 18 seconds. I stood in Red Square just outside the Kremlin and watched as an entourage of about 500 angels were dispatched all over Russia. I am not at liberty to divulge the prophetic word but I will give you a clue; look up Ezekiel chapters 38 and 39 and you will find out what I was called upon to do.

Thus this gift of prophecy never stops growing but keeps increasing in its anointing and impact. Expect these vocal gifts to grow and develop beyond the baby stage and stand in awe of what God will call upon you for.

If we are faithful in little God will make us ruler over much. These things come in stages like anything else in the kingdom. Simply take all of the steps that God gives you at this moment in time and then watch it grow. The anointing grows in stages in every area of our spiritual development so just be patient and faithful with all that He gives you and He will advance you when you are ready.

Chapter 13

The Gifts of Revelation and Power

I have found that the anointing upon these mighty gifts of the Holy Spirit has developed significantly over the years. They are so commonplace in my life now that I simply operate in these giftings quite naturally without even thinking about it. I remember when I first began to experience these gifts I would take special note of what had just taken place and I would often say something like 'that was a word of knowledge' for instance. Now I flow in them daily just as naturally as cleaning my teeth!

The Revelation Gifts

As we stated in the last chapter there are three gifts of revelation contained in the nine spiritual gifts. These are: a word of knowledge, a word of wisdom and discerning of spirits.

When you read about the first mentioned gift here in Scripture it says 'The word of knowledge'. This should read 'A word of knowledge'. The word 'the' is not in the Greek text. The translators added it to try to make more sense. It should read 'a'. This shows how accurate the Word of God is because there is no such thing as 'The word of knowledge'. We only ever have 'a' word from God about anything.

People often ask me how I know when I have received a word of knowledge. My answer is very simple. It is simply a passing thought that I have learned over the years to recognise. For example, I will be preaching at a meeting and all of a sudden a word will come into my mind such as 'headache' or 'cancer'. At a convenient moment I will call out these problems and people always respond. Sometimes I will have very detailed words about a condition which narrows things down. In the last 18 years I have hardly ever been wrong with the use of this gift. In fact I am so confident about it now that when this gifting comes upon me I do not rest until the people respond.

This happened very recently on my current trip here in the USA. I was preaching in a church and I had a word about sexual immorality, unclean thoughts and lust. I gave out the word and nobody responded. The Lord then told me that there were five such people who needed to be prayed for. I then had a word of wisdom about how to proceed. I asked everyone to close their eyes and for those five people to put up their hand. Five hands went up straight away and I then asked them to come out to the front. They all came out and were set free.

I get words of knowledge about all sorts of things. Financial situations, demons (frequently), territorial spirits over towns, cities or nations, sicknesses, diseases, infirmities, physical conditions, mental problems, unforgiveness etc. The Lord can use this gifting in every area of life. It is even used when you lose something. The word of knowledge gift can reveal where it is. If I forget something I will simply pray in the Holy Spirit for a couple of minutes and a word of knowledge reminds me. It is a wonderful gift that I could not survive without!

I am glad that it has developed so well over the years, to the point where I don't have to wait very long. This was not always the case! It used to take me a long time before I really broke through in this area, so be patient with God and yourself. Over the years I have fasted and prayed in the Spirit consistently which has contributed greatly to the efficiency of this and all the gifts of the Spirit.

I have often been asked what is the difference between a word of wisdom and a word of knowledge. Basically, a word of knowledge is a piece of information only. A word of wisdom is what to do with it. Someone once said that wisdom was the ability to handle knowledge. I would agree with this. For example, a word of knowledge would be 'there is someone in the meeting with cancer'. A word of wisdom would be 'tell the man with cancer that he will be healed as soon as he forgives his brother'. That is a word of instruction for the person. A word of wisdom would also be direction.

These gifts of the Spirit are often used by the Holy Spirit when someone is preaching under the anointing. They may not even be aware that something that they said was coming through them but the one listening certainly was! These words can come very casually also simply through general conversation. I have often been talking with someone and they have said a word or two that confirms things to me through them. This is how these gifts can work naturally.

Once a person has been born again and baptised with the Spirit with the evidence of speaking with tongues, then they are a candidate for all these gifts. Expect these things to happen to you.

The word of knowledge works hand in hand with the power gifts in particular. When I am praying for the sick or casting out devils (or both together!) I find that words of knowledge flow frequently to complement these miraculous gifts.

1 Corinthians 12:11 says:

> *'But all these worketh that one and the selfsame Spirit, dividing to every man severally as he will.'*

Many people have testified to starting off in these gifts by having a word of knowledge or wisdom in a seemingly trivial situation where there is no responsibility. I remember one of our members many years ago lost her bus ticket and needed it to get home one night. She looked everywhere but could not find it. Then she prayed and asked for a word from God and the Lord told her to look by the toilet. She went into the bathroom and there it was! This is how we learn to develop confidence in these gifts. It is the same with tongues and interpretation; you can speak out a message in tongues and interpret yourself on your own which helps to bring confidence in that gift also. This is how the anointing grows in this area of the Christian life. If you are faithful in little then the Lord will make you ruler over much. Just be faithful at what you are doing now and the Lord will advance you one step at a time. Many people want a **big** ministry but do not realise that we all have to take **all** the steps to reach our ultimate destiny. Be patient!

Discerning of Spirits

1 Corinthians 12:10 says:

> *'To another the working of miracles; to another prophecy; **to another discerning of spirits**; to another divers kinds of tongues; to another the interpretation of tongues.'*

Notice that it does not say the gift of discernment. There is no such 'gift'. Discernment is something that we all have to a greater or lesser extent. The closer we are to the Lord the sharper our discernment is about everything in life. For instance: where to give our money, what relationships to make, who to marry, who to associate with in business, which church to go to etc. Discernment is part of the fruit of the Spirit of wisdom. We base our decisions in life on the quality of our discernment of people and situations.

This is not discerning of spirits. The spiritual gift of discerning of spirits is a specific gift to reveal the operation of evil spirits only. That is all it is for. God has placed a strong emphasis in the church regarding demons by allocating a whole spiritual gift to discerning them. This gift does not cast out demons, it simply locates them.

Many years ago I asked my pastor, Aubrey Whittall (who is still my pastor), about the whole subject of deliverance and casting out demons. I knew absolutely nothing about this subject and wanted to understand it just in case I ever came into contact with demons in my ministry. I did not know what I was letting myself in for! He sat me down and taught me for a lesson every week for about 10 weeks or so. I just drank in from this man of God who had a great wealth of experience in this area of ministry. He told me stories that caused goose bumps all down my back. I later discovered that this ministry of deliverance was a very controversial subject amongst Pentecostal people as well as many denominations.

From the very first lesson that he taught me I was gripped

with compassion for those who were bound in any way and desired to set them free in the name of Jesus Christ.

Then someone in our church came to me with a problem and I knew it was demonic in nature. I cast out the devil and the person never had that problem again. Wow! This is real.

Aubrey then told me about the gift of discerning of spirits and how it works. I certainly wanted this gift. I was all ears! He told me that this gift operated through his left hand. An anointing would come upon him right in the centre of his left hand like a dull ache. As he described this gifting to me I started to feel my hands begin to tingle. Something I had never felt before. Then, a deep anointing came into my left hand just like he said. I have experienced this anointing so much that it has become part of my every day life. He said that each time this anointing would come upon him he would have to cast out devils within 24 hours. The same thing began to happen with me. The anointing would come into my left hand and then someone would need ministry or the telephone would ring and I would know that the person's need was demonic. It was great. It was never wrong. In fact I can honestly say before God that every time without exception that this anointing has come upon me I have to minister deliverance to others or, more recently, impart this gifting into other people's lives.

I was in a service just last night in the USA where I am ministering, and I prayed for about 350 people for healing and deliverance. As soon as I touched some of them they began to manifest demons and I cast out the spirits in the Name of Jesus Christ. One lady was very violent and it took about three men to hold her down as I cast out many strong occult devils out of her.

The anointing in this area of ministry has grown steadily over the years and I am called on more and more to cast out demons all over the world.

In our church in Stoke-on-Trent, England, we were experiencing so many people coming for deliverance that I prayed about it and God told me to set up a school of deliverance. We have a session every two weeks on a Monday night just for deliverance from demonic spirits. This has been so successful that we now have people coming from different parts of the country and even as far away as Switzerland, seeking to be set free from evil spirits.

If you would like to know more about this ministry then please write to us and order our book called *Angels, Demons and Spiritual Warfare*. This is our best-selling book and will answer most, if not all your questions.

A few years ago the Lord spoke to me and said 'You are now well established in the power gifts and revelation gifts and I want you to share these giftings with others and impart them to those that I will send to you.' I was awed by this and did a study in imparting gifts to others. Look at the following scriptures:

> *'For I long to see you, that I may impart unto you some spiritual gift, to the end ye may be established.'*
>
> (Romans 1:11)

> *'Neglect not the gift that is in thee, which was given thee by prophecy, with the laying on of the hands of the presbytery.'*
>
> (1 Timothy 4:14)

> *'As every man hath received the gift, even so minister the same one to another, as good stewards of the manifold grace of God.'* (1 Peter 4:10)

I quickly realised that spiritual gifts could be imparted to others and that this anointing could be transferred. A few weeks later someone came to me and I was prompted by the Lord to impart these gifts to them. I obeyed and the exact anointing that was upon my life came upon them. In fact, I have imparted these gifts to many people and the same anointing comes upon everyone as it works through me. This is how to multiply the gifting throughout the body. We are not to keep these treasures to ourselves but rather to expand the ministry so that more can be ministered to. Delegation works for everything. What is more, as I share this anointing with others, in turn my anointing grows and flourishes. I know that if I kept it all to myself then I would stagnate and only see a little fruit. It is also the law of sowing and reaping. Once you are established in anything in the kingdom of God then you are required to share and impart to others.

2 Timothy 2:2 says:

> *'And the things that thou hast heard of me among many witnesses, the same commit thou to faithful men, who shall be able to teach others also.'*

The Gifts of Healings

> *'To another faith by the same Spirit; to another the gifts of healing by the same Spirit.'*   (1 Corinthians 12:9)

> *'Have all the gifts of healing? do all speak with tongues? do all interpret?'*   (1 Corinthians 12:30)

> *'And God hath set some in the church, first apostles, secondarily prophets, thirdly teachers, after that miracles, then gifts of healings, helps, governments, diversities of tongues.'*   (1 Corinthians 12:28)

You will notice that it is not the gift of healing singular but 'gifts' of 'healings'. One translation says healings in both 1 Corinthians 12:9, 30 which is substantiated in some Greek dictionaries.

I have heard different theories about why it is plural and would not want to argue about any of them since they all may be correct. I once heard someone say that there are many ways to understand certain truths in Scripture as there are many sides on a diamond.

For instance, some people have testified in their healing ministry that God uses them in healing certain sicknesses more than others. I was talking to a dear friend in ministry who said that his mother was well-known for her healing in the area of cancer. Apparently every cancer case that she prayed for was healed without exception. Hallelujah! I believe it with all of my heart. This same pastor then told me that he had a strong anointing to pray for deaf people. This of course does not mean that these are the only conditions that they will pray for but that they have special anointing in certain areas. I have noticed recently in my own healing ministry that God seems to use me a lot to bring healing to people with feet and leg conditions. I could not say that this is the only way that I am used but I do find myself praying for these conditions frequently.

The Amplified Bible translates the gifts of healing as follows:

'The extraordinary powers of healing.'

(in both verses 9 and 30)

This is one of the most graphic anointings to draw attention to the gospel of Jesus Christ. We need to pray for this gifting to rise more and more in the body of Christ. Jesus Himself was used greatly in the ministry of healing which drew large crowds to hear what He had to say.

Matthew 4:23–25 says:

> *'And Jesus went about all Galilee, teaching in their synagogues, and preaching the gospel of the kingdom, and healing all manner of sickness and all manner of disease among the people. And his fame went throughout all Syria: and they brought unto him all sick people that were taken with divers diseases and torments, and those which were possessed with devils, and those which were lunatick, and those that had the palsy; and he healed them. And there followed him great multitudes of people from Galilee, and from Decapolis, and from Jerusalem, and from Judaea, and from beyond Jordan.'*

Healing is the fastest way to create interest in Christianity. Jesus set us the example and we should follow it. I have always sought after the gifts of healing for the sake of the kingdom and over the years the anointing has grown in stages. There is a price to be paid for spiritual power. Many want to heal the sick but are not prepared to pay the high price for that power. Whenever you see a tremendous ministry always remember that they did not begin at that level of anointing. They have had to grow just like everybody else. There is nothing special about that person! They will have spent much time seeking God in their private devotion, had many seasons of prayer and fasting, faced huge levels of persecution and verbal abuse, been let down many times, rejected, misunderstood, felt lonely, been discouraged etc. If you think for one moment that having a healing ministry is the most glamorous life on earth then grow up! Only the tough survive in this kind of anointing. If ever the Lord leads you into a healing ministry then stay alert at all times because you will have to face attacks against you that you never had to face before. If you are going to be successful in a healing ministry then the whole of your life needs to be in order.

Your character is very important. Your attitudes and motives need to be pure. Honesty, integrity and truth need to be high on your list of priorities. Find out what your weaknesses are and avoid them. Satan does not just attack your weaknesses but also your strengths. We often relax in our strong points because we think we are immune from attack. Just because you have a strong marriage does not mean that you are immune from sexual temptation. We need to be on our guard in every area of life at all times and to take heed to the Holy Spirit's warnings. He will warn you if you need it. One person said that your wife is like the second Holy Spirit. If the Holy Spirit doesn't remind you then your wife will! I thank God for my wife. We need to listen to our wives more. The greater the anointing, the greater the attacks! Remember that.

Over the years I have noticed that the Father in His wisdom has released the healing anointing into my life one step at a time. Even though I have prepared myself for this gifting in every way possible it has seemed a slow process. I have longed to see tremendous healings every time I touch people. However, I understand more now as to why this particular anointing takes time to develop. One of the main reasons is that **it brings attention to you**! Many do not cope very well with this and it can feed pride etc. God does not want us to be destroyed through pride and so He leads us one step at a time. I used to want it all at once but I have now learned after watching many ministries fall over the years that it is better to grow slowly than too quickly. I have learned to be a tortoise rather than the hare!

During 1997 the Lord spoke to me regarding the healing anointing and said to me that I was going to experience a greater anointing in 1998 than ever before. For the first half of 1998 I did not see any major breakthroughs and then things started to happen. In the last few months I have seen some of the most powerful healing miracles of my life and I want it to continue!

I have stood in faith to walk in the same anointing for healing as Jesus Christ Himself. He said that we could and so I believe it. The believing is our part. The manifestation is up to God. He will release these mighty gifts when He knows that we can handle it and not before. I have been aware of going through a season of testing when I knew that the Lord was doing a thorough check on my attitudes, motives etc. Increase has come. Hallelujah!

What would we do in ministry without the anointing of the Holy Spirit?

I would now like to describe the anointing that I have for healing the sick. The anointing is a heat in my right hand which is the same as my pastor. People often say that they can feel a heat enter them as soon as someone lays hands on them. I can often feel heat leave my hand as soon as I touch them. I am sure that others could testify to other manifestations but that is what happens with me and many others that I have shared with. This will help you to identify these giftings if ever you experience these different anointings of the Holy Spirit. Many do not know what they are until someone tells them.

Chapter 14

Working of Miracles

1 Corinthians 12:10 says:

> *'To another the working of miracles; to another prophecy; to another discerning of spirits; to another divers kinds of tongues; to another the interpretation of tongues.'*

The gift of the Spirit called 'working of miracles' is used for different purposes one of which is in the area of healing where the gift of healing does not cover. For example, the gifts of healings would be called upon to heal someone who was sick but the working of miracles would be used to recreate a part of someone's body. There are times when a part of the body no longer functions properly and so God has put this gift of working of miracles into the church for such an occasion. Many people have testified to having new parts replaced – even teeth! I once had a tooth replaced in answer to prayer. I once prayed for a man who had had epilepsy and had been left with brain damage. As I prayed for him he said he could feel heat in his head and literally felt his brain being recreated. He always used to walk crooked but after prayer could walk straight.

There are other reasons for the gift of working of miracles that I have experienced over the years. Whenever I pray for those who need the baptism in the Spirit I feel my hands tingling with the anointing of the Spirit. Both my hands tingle when I am used in this gifting. I have prayed for thousands of people to receive this baptism in the Spirit with great success, to the glory of God. One time in Argentina I gave an appeal for anyone who wanted to be baptised in the Spirit and 120 people responded. I told the counsellors not to lay hands on the people. I simply prayed knowing the anointing in my hands and about 115 came through speaking in tongues in about three minutes! The others needed deliverance which we sorted out and then I prayed again and they all came through. The leaders were astonished at the results. This is the power of this gift! Praise God.

I also have the working of miracles when I am casting out demons on a regular basis. The ministry of deliverance utilises many of the spiritual gifts and is one of the most anointed areas of ministry. My hands usually tingle with the anointing an hour or so before I have to minister deliverance.

Whenever I am called upon to impart spiritual gifts to others I always have this gift of working of miracles. The Lord uses this gift to transfer other gifts through me to others. This happens quite often particularly when I minister to ministers.

The other time that I sense the working of miracles gift is when I have a personal prophecy for someone.

Consequently, as soon as this anointing comes upon me I know that I have to do one or more of the above spiritual activities. At the moment I am preaching for four weeks in America and so these gifts have been called upon very much often in quick succession. One meeting finishes and I am preparing for another. My hands are being anointed all the time during such intense times of ministry. It is so common now that I hardly even notice it. These power gifts are so normal to me that I just do it.

When you read through the Gospels you will be able to identify which gifts Jesus was being used in much more after reading this book. You will become aware that when He prayed for someone He was often moving in more than one anointing. Healing and deliverance are so close that some-times Jesus would cast out a demon through a word of knowledge and then pray a prayer of healing. He did it so naturally and quickly that we often miss what is actually going on. I appreciate this more and more as I have to minister in the power of the Spirit to more and more people.

The Gift of Faith

You will notice that faith is the only commodity mentioned in both the fruit and gifts of the Spirit. However, it is referring to something different. In the fruit of the Spirit it is dealing with the faith that we have all the time which simply grows as we use it. The gift of faith is quite different. I had always wanted to be used in this gift and cried out to God for it to help mankind. I knew that if ever I was confronted with certain situations that the only thing that would help would be this gifting. I had read about Smith Wigglesworth trying to raise a man from the dead. He told the corpse to come back to life, but to no avail. He did it several times and then an overwhelming sense of faith came over him from his stomach and he 'knew' that when he spoke this time the man would come alive. Sure enough with this supernatural level of faith the man was raised from the dead. I never forgot that story and waited for the day when I would be called upon to do something like that. I would often visualise what I would do and go over it again and again in my mind.

One day in Manchester we were having a service and I was leading the worship that day. I had a word of knowledge and gave it out. The word was 'quadriplegia' which of course is total paralysis. I asked the person to put their hand up in response to the word not realising what I was saying! Nobody responded and I just continued with the meeting. Then a few minutes later I opened my eyes and saw a lady in a wheel-chair being prayed for by our leadership team. The Lord spoke to me and told me to pull her out of the chair. I waited for a few moments and I remembered the anointing that Smith Wigglesworth talked about in his stomach. At that moment I felt a surge of Divine power go through my stomach and I knew it was this gift of faith. I went up to her and commanded her to get up. She did and the power of God healed her instantly. She walked with me around the church and then I asked her if she was born again. She said 'no' so I asked her if she wanted to get saved and she did. The church went wild with excitement. Then I found out that she had been brought to our church by her mother who was a spiritualist! She had tried to get her healed at the spiritualist church for years with no help at all. But the first time she came to a real church of Jesus Christ the power of God healed her and saved her.

This is the gift of faith. It is the instantaneous miracle power of God used for these kinds of situations. Raising the dead, pulling people out of wheelchairs, etc.

I remember one man testifying to a situation regarding the obvious use of this gift. A preacher was once standing at the bottom of a block of offices when all of a sudden a man fell to the ground on his head. His head split open causing an awful mess on the pavement. He died instantly. However, this preacher reached down and lifted up his head from the floor and commanded him to be made whole. In front of many people the Lord miraculously put the man's head back together and raised him from the dead in a moment of time. This is the gift of faith.

Many years ago a man by the name of Jack Coe was holding a healing service and there were 22 people in wheel-chairs all in a row. With the help of the gift of faith this man of God went along and pulled each one out of the chair in the name of Jesus and 20 of them were instantly healed. To my knowledge this is the most graphic example of the gift of faith on record in modern times. Please agree with me in prayer that this gifting would be fully restored to the church today for the demonstration of God's power to the world. We need these gifts more and more if we are to see revival.

Every born-again Spirit-filled Christian can be used in these gifts. Ask God today for these gifts to help mankind in their suffering.

1 Corinthians 14:1 says:

> *'Follow after charity, and* **desire spiritual gifts**, *but rather that ye may prophesy.'*

If you desire these gifts then the Lord will respond to your expectation.

One translation says, *'covet earnestly spiritual gifts'*.

Chapter 15

Jesus Christ the Anointed One!

The word 'Christ' actually means 'anointed' or 'anointing'. Therefore, Jesus Christ can also mean Jesus the Anointed and His Anointing!

As we develop a close personal relationship with Jesus Christ then we will automatically grow up in the anointing of the Holy Spirit. Every time we witness to people about Jesus the Anointed one then we will grow in that anointing. In fact every time we use His Name in prayer we are being exercised in the anointing!

As a preacher I am very aware of the awesome anointing that accompanies ministering the Word of God. The anointing I often feel when preaching is like nothing else on earth.

I have noticed that there are different anointings upon different subjects when teaching and preaching. Whenever I teach or preach on faith there are usually two things that happen. The first thing is the attacks from the devil and secondly the awesome anointing upon me when I actually preach! When I speak on the Second Coming of Christ there is a particular anointing that is unique to that subject. This is just an observation that I have noticed over the years.

Many of you reading this book may think that the anointing is largely reserved for preachers! Well that is not the case at all. In fact there is an anointing upon every task in the kingdom of God. Take a look at the following scriptures:

> 'And he hath filled him with the spirit of God, in wisdom, in understanding, and in knowledge, and in all manner of

workmanship; And to devise curious works, to work in gold,
and in silver, and in brass, And in the cutting of stones, to set
them, and in carving of wood, to make any manner of
cunning work.'   (Exodus 35:31–33)

These tasks are all important in the work of God but each
one demanded an anointing to do those duties. So it is today
in the church. As a pastor I want the right people doing the
right tasks who are anointed to do those duties. There are
some duties that have to have someone anointed to do them
right. The people who lead worship for instance need to be
anointed. It is not enough just to be good musicians! In fact if
I have the choice between having a professional musician
who is not anointed and someone who only just plays
but who is anointed then I will always choose the one who
is anointed. The church does not need professionals but
those who are anointed. Having said that, just because you
may be a professional musician does not mean that you
cannot have an anointing to lead music. That would be
wonderful! Sadly, I have seen all too often professional
singers and musicians at major Christian events who lack
the anointing.

In the area of administration and office skills I want
someone who is called to it and has the anointing upon
them. These are vital positions in the church and should not
be given to those who are not meant to be doing them.

I believe that God provides for His church all the right
giftings to fulfil the local vision and we need to find out
about all the gifts that He sends us so that we can release
them. The church is a body made up of many members all
functioning in their differing callings.

Every time I listen to a preacher I am looking for one thing.
The vital ingredient! If a person is not anointed to preach
then they should sit down. We do not want professionals in
the pulpit but prophets! Men and women who know God
and have met with Him. The anointing of God separates
people for special tasks of service. We need anointed people
who are full of the mighty Spirit of the living God to change
this world of ours from darkness to light and from the power
of Satan to God.

Don't seek to have your head filled with theology. Seek the Lord for a mighty anointing of the Holy Spirit so that you will become a vessel in the hand of God to transform lives. It is the anointing that makes all the difference!

- The anointing **sets you apart from the crowd.**
- The anointing **produces fruit that remains.**
- The anointing **makes ordinary people special.**
- The anointing **destroys the yoke of bondage.**
- The anointing **causes a reaction in the spirit world.**
- The anointing **provokes the devil.**
- The anointing **upsets religious spirits and traditions of men.**
- The anointing **always attracts persecution.**
- The anointing **is a manifestation of God's Glory.**
- The anointing **changes lives.**
- The anointing **makes you shine out instead of blend in.**
- The anointing **makes people sit up and listen.**
- The anointing **removes boredom from the church.**
- The anointing **creates excitement.**
- The anointing **brings people to Jesus Christ.**
- The anointing **causes sick bodies to be healed.**
- The anointing **changes a song into an anthem of worship.**

Don't settle for mediocre, wishy-washy, sugar-coated, life-less religion when you can have a demonstration of the power of God with an ever increasing manifestation of His Divine Presence in your life.

Seek to live your Christian life on the cutting edge of the anointing at all times to bring honour, glory and majesty to the King of kings and Lord of lords.

Romans 15:19 says:

> *'Through mighty signs and wonders, by the power of the Spirit of God; so that from Jerusalem, and round about unto Illyricum, I have fully preached the gospel of Christ.'*

I pray that you grow in the anointing of the Spirit in every area of your life and that you find out where your particular anointings are within the body. God bless you richly in your service for the Master.

1 John 2:27 says:

> *'But the anointing which ye have received of him abideth in you, and ye need not that any man teach you: but as the same anointing teacheth you of all things, and is truth, and is no lie, and even as it hath taught you, ye shall abide in him.'*

Other books by Trevor Newport

What the Bible says about YOUR Provision and Prosperity
Did you go OR were you sent? (An autobiography)
King Jesus is Coming Soon!
Angels, Demons and Spiritual Warfare
The Ministry of Jesus Christ
Divine Appointments
The Two U's: Unbelief and Unforgiveness
Secrets of Success
From Victory to Victory
Pitfalls in Ministry
How to Pray in the Spirit

For more information about any aspect of this ministry
please contact:

Life-Changing Ministries
Bemersley House
Gitana Street
Hanley
Stoke-on-Trent
Staffordshire
ST1 1DY
England

Phone/Fax: 01782 272 671
(*overseas*: +44 1782 272 671)

Website: www.lcm.clara.net